Contents

CW00349707

Introduction

For the teacher

Supporting Number has been written to support teaching assistants working with lower-ability children from Reception to Year 6. Each book contains 55 2-page teaching units which address the earlier objectives from the relevant NNS yearly teaching programme. The combination of practical activities and guidance helps to ensure that children get maximum benefit from the presence of an additional adult, while the easy-to-use photocopiable format includes space for the teaching assistant to provide you with focused feedback on children's strengths and weaknesses.

Discuss these lessons with the teaching assistant and involve them in planning where possible. It is intended that the activities follow your oral/mental starter and the whole-class teaching input. Encourage children from the teaching assistant's group to report back to the class during the plenary. The activities within a unit can be extended across more than one day and can be repeated throughout the year to further consolidate the mathematical ideas and help to prevent children from falling behind.

The teaching units follow the order suggested by the NNS *Sample medium-term plans for mathematics* (see pages 6–8). However, given that this is only a sample plan, the broader match to the *Framework* on page 9 lists all the units that relate to each content area, giving you the flexibility to deal with topics in a different order, and enabling you to find related activities.

For the teaching assistant

The teaching units contained in this book give information on:

▸ resources needed in the lesson
▸ words to use – appropriate vocabulary for children of this age and ability range
▸ things to note – points to watch for and to be aware of relating to language, mathematical skills and knowledge, and potential difficulties
▸ what to do – the activities, with questions to ask
▸ feedback – specific questions with space for you to write notes on the children's achievements, difficulties, and any other points of interest. This information can be of great value in providing the teacher with a detailed record of the children's work with you and helping them to plan more effectively for future lessons.

Maths doesn't have to be hard!

Many children find maths difficult and, as a result, can become anxious and negative towards it. Maths builds up in a way that means certain things need to be understood before sense can be made of what comes next, particularly in the case of number work. Numbers to 5 are learnt before numbers to 50, for example, and addition comes before multiplication. If children are moved too quickly, they often fail to really understand and so fall behind. Many children need help and support to overcome their difficulties if they are to become confident with maths both in and out of school.

It's good to talk

Talking about maths is an excellent way of coming to understand it. Choosing words carefully and explaining things logically can help us to understand more clearly. It can also help others who are listening and responding to clarify their understanding.

Supporting Number

Activities for Teaching Assistants

Steve Mills and Hilary Koll

Halley Court, Jordan Hill, Oxford, OX2 8EJ
a division of Reed Educational and Professional Publishing Ltd
www.heinemann.co.uk

Heinemann is a registered trademark of Reed Educational and Professional Publishing Ltd

© Steve Mills and Hilary Koll 2000

The material in the publication is copyright. The Photocopy Masters may be photocopied for one-time use as instructional material in a classroom, but they may not be copied in unlimited quantities, kept on behalf of others, passed on or sold to third parties, or stored for future use in a retrieval system. If you wish to use the material in any other way than that specified you must apply in writing to the Publisher.

The text on pages 6–8 is taken from the NNS *Sample medium-term plans for mathematics*, published by the DfEE. Crown copyright is reproduced with the permission of the Controller of Her Majesty's Stationery Office.

ISBN 0 435 03266 6

04   03   02   01   00
10 9 8 7 6 5 4 3 2

Typeset by Artistix
Illustrated by Nick Schon
Printed and bound in Great Britain by Page Bros.

Children can be encouraged to talk about the maths they are doing in several ways:

Asking children to explain
- asking a child to explain how they worked something out
- asking children to suggest alternative strategies
- asking children to explain what they have done so far
- asking children to explain what they have done to a friend

As children discuss their work they will make mistakes. Try to avoid saying *No, that's wrong*, as doing so can make children reluctant to offer ideas next time. Instead, ask *How did you get that? Why do you think that?* or *Do we all agree?*

Listen carefully to children's explanations. They can tell you a lot about whether a child really understands. Encourage the other children to listen carefully, too.

Questioning
There are two types of question you can ask children. The first type, closed questions, have only one answer, for example *Three plus two equals …?* or *What are five sixes?* The second kind are called open questions and have more than one answer, for example *Tell me two numbers that add up to five.*

Here are some examples of both, showing how a closed question can be 'opened out':

Closed questions	Open questions
$6 + 4 = ?$ ⟶	*What pairs of numbers add to make 10?*
$5 - 2 = ?$ ⟶	*Give me two numbers with a difference of 3.*
Is 6 an even number? ⟶	*Tell me some even numbers you know.*

Asking an open question can tell you more about what a child understands than a closed one. For example, *What is 17 minus 5?* allows Jo to show you that she can do $17 - 5$. But that's all. She may be capable of $100 - 88$, but has no opportunity to show you. Closed questions put a ceiling on what a child can show. Open questions remove the ceiling, allowing children to really demonstrate what they can do:

If the answer is 12, what could the question be?

Questions can be asked at various times during an activity:

At the beginning *What do you have to do?* *What are you going to use?* *What do you think the answer might roughly be?*	**During** *Why did you choose to do it this way?* *What will you do next?* *Is there a quicker way?* *Can you see a pattern?*
If children get stuck *What have you done so far?* *Would some cubes/pictures etc. help?* *What did we do yesterday?* *Can anyone else help him?*	**After** *How did you work it out?* *How did you check your answer?* *What new words have you learnt?* *What must you remember for tomorrow?*

Match to NNS Sample medium-term plan for Reception

AUTUMN TERM

NNS unit	NNS pages	Topic	Objectives; children will be taught to:	Teaching unit
1	2–8	Counting	Say and use number names to 5 in order in familiar contexts, e.g. number rhymes, songs, stories.	1
			Recite number names in order from 1 up to 5.	2
2	2–8	Counting	Say and use number names to 10 in order in familiar contexts, e.g. number rhymes, songs, stories.	3
			Recite number names in order from 1 up to 10.	4
			Count reliably up to 3 objects.	
3	24–7	Shape and space	Use language such as *round, circle, square* to describe shapes.	
			Use words such as *bigger* and *smaller* to describe size.	
			Use shapes to make pictures and patterns.	
4	2–8	Counting	Count reliably up to 5 objects.	5
	22–3	Measures	Use more or less, longer or shorter to make direct comparisons of two lengths.	
5	2–8	Counting	Begin to recognize none and zero in stories and rhymes.	6
	14–15	Adding (one more)	Find one more than (up to 5 objects).	7
6		Assess and review		
7	2–8	Counting	Say and use number names to 10 in order in familiar contexts, e.g. number rhymes, songs, stories.	8
			Recite number names in order from 1 up to 20.	9
	11–13	Comparing and ordering numbers	Use language such as *more* and *less, greater* or *smaller* to compare two numbers up to 5 and say which is more or less.	10
8	2–8	Counting	Recite number names in order from 1 to 20 and beyond.	11
			Count reliably more than 5 objects.	12
	14–15	Adding and subtracting (one more, one less)	Find *one more* or *one less* than a number up to 9.	13
9	24–7	Shape and space	Name solids: *cube, sphere, cone.*	
			Put sets of objects in order of size.	
			Use everyday words to describe position.	
	18–19	Reasoning	Talk about and recognise simple symmetrical patterns.	
10	2–8	Counting	Count reliably up to 10 objects.	14
	22–3	Measures, including time	Use language such as *more* or *less, heavier* or *lighter* to make direct comparisons of two lengths or masses.	
			Fill and empty containers, using words such as *full, empty, holds more, holds less.*	
			Begin to use vocabulary of time.	
			Sequence familiar events.	
11	2–8	Counting	Count reliably up to 10 objects or clapping sounds.	15
	20–21	Money and 'real life' problems	Recognize 1p coins.	16
			Solve practical problems involving counting in 'real life' or role play.	
			Sort and match objects.	
12		Assess and review		

SPRING TERM

NNS unit	NNS pages	Topic	Objectives; children will be taught to:	Teaching unit
1	2–8	Counting	Say and use number names beyond 10 in order in familiar contexts, e.g. number rhymes, songs, stories.	17
			Recite number names in order, continuing from 2, 3 or 4.	18
	11–13	Comparing and ordering numbers	Order a given set of numbers (e.g. 1–6 given in random order).	19
2	2–8	Counting	Count reliably up to 12 objects.	20
	14–17	Adding and subtracting	Begin to use the language involved in adding.	21
			Begin to relate addition to combining two groups of objects, counting all the objects.	
			Separate (partition) a given number of objects into 2 groups.	22
3	24–7	Shape and space	Begin to name solids and flat shapes.	
			Use shapes to describe and make models, pictures, patterns.	
	18–19	Reasoning	Solve simple problems or puzzles in a practical context.	
			Match objects (shapes).	
4	2–8	Counting	Recite the number names in order, counting back from 6, 5 or 4.	23
	22–3	Measures	Use language such as *more* or *less, longer* or *shorter, heavier* or *lighter* (length, mass, time) to make direct comparisons of two quantities.	
5	2–8	Counting	Count reliably up to 12 objects, claps or hops.	24
	14–17	Adding and subtracting	Begin to use the language involved in subtracting.	25
			Relate subtraction to taking away, counting how many are left.	
	19–20	Money and 'real life' problems	Sort coins: 1p, 2p, 5p.	26
6		Assess and review		
7	2–9	Counting and reading numbers	Say and use number names up to 20 in order in familiar contexts, e.g. number rhymes, songs, stories.	
			Recognize numerals 1 to 3.	27
	11–13	Comparing and ordering numbers	Compare two numbers. Say a number that lies between two given numbers up to 10 (then beyond).	28
8	2–9	Counting and reading numbers	Count reliably up to 15.	29
			Recognize numerals 1 to 5.	
			Recognize small numbers without counting.	
	14–17	Adding and subtracting	Relate addition to combining 2, then 3 groups.	30
			Relate addition to counting on.	31
9	24–7 18–19	Shape and space Reasoning	Talk about, recognize and recreate simple patterns, including patterns in the environment.	
	24–7	Shape and space	Use everyday words to describe position and direction.	
10	2–9	Counting and reading numbers	Recite the number names in order, counting on or back from 10 or 9.	32
			Recognize numerals 1 to 9.	33
	22–3	Measures, including time	Make direct comparisons of 2 then 3 or more lengths or masses.	
			Know the days of the week in order.	
11	2–9	Counting and reading numbers	Count reliably to 20.	34
			Recognize numerals 0 to 9.	
	14–17	Adding and subtracting	Relate addition to counting on.	35
	20–21	Money and 'real life' problems	Understand and use the vocabulary related to money.	36
			Sort coins: 1p, 2p, 5p, 10p, 20p. Use 1p coins in role play.	
			Sort and match objects, justifying decisions made.	
12		Assess and review		

SUMMER TERM

NNS unit	NNS pages	Topic	Objectives; children will be taught to:	Teaching unit
1	2–10	Counting, reading and writing numbers	Say and use number names beyond 20 in order in contexts, e.g. number rhymes, songs, counting games and activities.	37
	11–13	Comparing and ordering numbers	Order a given set of selected numbers, e.g. 2, 5, 8, 1, 4.	38
2	2–10	Counting, reading and writing numbers	Count reliably to 20 and beyond (objects and other contexts).	
			Recognize numerals 0 to 10.	39
			Record numbers by making marks.	
	14–17	Adding and subtracting	Begin to relate addition of doubles to counting on.	40
			Find a total by counting on when one group is hidden.	
3	24–7	Shape and space	Talk about and recreate symmetrical patterns found in the environment and in different cultures.	
	18–19	Reasoning	Make simple estimates and predictions.	
4	2–10	Counting, reading and writing numbers	Write numerals to 5.	41
			Count and record larger numbers by tallying.	42
	22–3	Measures	Compare lengths, masses and capacities by direct comparison.	
5	2–10	Counting, reading and writing numbers	Count in tens.	43
			Recognize numerals beyond 10.	44
	14–17	Adding and subtracting	Remove a smaller number from a larger and find how many are left by counting back from the larger number.	45
	20–21	Money and 'real life' problems	Sort all coins, including £1 and £2, and use in role play.	46
			Solve practical problems.	
6		Assess and review		
7	2–10	Counting, reading and writing numbers	Estimate a number up to 10 and check by counting.	47
			Write numerals to 10.	
	11–13	Comparing and ordering numbers	Begin to understand and use ordinal numbers in different contexts.	48
8	2–10	Counting, reading and writing numbers	Count in twos.	49
	14–17	Adding and subtracting	Select two groups of objects to make a given total.	
			Begin to find how many have been removed from a group of objects by counting up from a number.	50
9	24–7	Shape and space	Use everyday words to describe position, direction and movement.	
	18–19	Reasoning	Sort and match objects, shapes and pictures, justifying the decisions made.	
10	2–10	Counting, reading and writing numbers	Begin to write numerals to 20.	51
			Estimate a number beyond 10 and check by counting.	52
	22–3	Measures, including time	Begin to read *o'clock* time.	
11	2–10	Counting, reading and writing numbers	Count in tens.	53
			Count beyond 20 in twos.	
			Use numerals to record numbers.	
	14–17	Adding and subtracting	Work out by counting how many more are needed to make a larger number.	54
	19–20	Money and 'real life' problems	Use coins in role play to pay and give change.	55
			Make simple estimates and predictions.	
12		Assess and review		

NNS overview and match to *Mathematics 5–14*

Match to NNS *Framework for teaching Mathematics* for Reception

Strand	Topic	Teaching unit
Counting and recognizing numbers	Number names	1, 2, 3, 4, 6, 8, 9, 11, 17, 18, 23, 32, 37
	Counting objects	4, 5, 12, 14, 15, 20, 24, 29, 34
	Counting in other contexts	15, 24
	Counting in tens/twos	43, 49, 53
	Estimating	47, 52
	Recognizing and recording numerals	27, 29, 33, 39, 41, 42, 44, 51
	Comparing numbers	10, 28
	Ordering numbers	19, 38
	Ordinal numbers	48
Adding and subtracting	Using vocabulary	21, 25, 30, 31
	Finding one more or one less	7, 13
	Addition by combining two groups	21, 30
	Addition by counting on	31, 35, 40, 21, 30
	Partitioning objects into two groups	22
	Selecting groups of objects to make a total	21, 30
	Subtracting as 'taking away'	25
	Subtracting by counting back	45
	Subtraction by counting up	50, 54
Solving problems	Making estimates and predictions	47, 52
	Solving practical problems	16
	Vocabulary related to money	26, 36, 46, 55

Match to *Mathematics 5–14*, Level A

	Strand	Level A	Teaching unit
Information handling	Collect	By obtaining information for a task from a picture, video or story;	1, 3, 8, 12, 17, 27, 37
		By collecting information about themselves and familar objects.	5, 14
	Organize	By tallying as collections of objects;	42
		By counting;	5, 10, 12, 14, 15, 20, 24, 28, 29, 30, 34, 39
		By sorting into specific sets (shape, colour, texture).	5, 6, 12, 15, 26, 36, 46, 55
	Display	By using real objects;	1, 5
		By using pictures;	12, 20
		By drawing simple diagrams such as one-to-one mappings.	
	Interpret	From displays by locating and counting.	8, 12, 15
Number, money and measurement	Range and type of numbers	Work with: – whole numbers 0 to 20 (count, order, read/write statements, display on calculator);	1, 2, 3, 4, 5, 6, 7, 8, 9, 10, 11, 12, 13, 14, 15, 16, 17, 18, 19, 20, 23, 24, 27, 28, 29, 31, 32, 33, 34, 37, 38, 39, 41, 42, 44, 47, 48, 51, 52
		– halves (practical applications only).	
	Money	Use 1p, 2p, 5p, 10p, 20p coins to buy things.	36, 46, 55
	Add and subtract	Add and subtract: – mentally for numbers 0 to 10,	7, 13, 21, 22, 25, 30, 31, 35, 40, 45, 50, 54
		– in applications in number, measurement and money, including payments and change to 10p.	
	Patterns and sequences	Work with patterns and sequences: – simple number sequences; – copy, continue and describe simple patterns or sequences of objects of different shape of colour.	23, 43, 49, 53

1 Counting

Objective

Say and use number names to five in order in familiar contexts such as number rhymes, songs, stories.

Resources

▸ objects for counting such as teddy bears, shoe laces, farm animals

What children are learning

familiarity with the rhythm and sound of the number names in order from one to five

Words you can use

count, number, one, two, three, four, five

Things to note

▸ Children need plenty of opportunity to hear and recite the number names in order. Saying the rhymes together can help children who lack confidence.
▸ Any number rhymes, songs or stories can be used for this lesson. Choose any that children enjoy and are familiar with within the number range 1–5. Titles of further number rhymes and stories can be found on the NNS CD-ROM (sent to schools during spring 2000).
▸ Children are not expected to be able to count five objects at this stage.

Activities

❶ Counting rhymes.
▸ Use pictures and objects as props while saying simple number rhymes aloud. Use a range of different sized and shaped things, for example fingers, teddy bears, shoe laces etc. The following rhyme can be adapted for each object or picture.

*I've got five **fingers**, pointing to the sky, now I'm going to count them, will you have a try? One, two, three, four, five.*

*Here are five **teddy bears**, sitting side by side, now I'm going to count them, will you have a try? One, two, three, four, five.*

*Here are five **aeroplanes**, flying way up high …*
*Here are five **shoe laces**, ready to be tied …*
*I can see five **lollies**, which one shall I buy? …*
*Here are five **piglets**, standing in their sty …*

‣ For each rhyme, discuss the items and invite children to join in with the rhymes as you say them. Point to each item as you say the number names to five.

‣ Choose a child to point to the items as they are counted. Ask individual children if they would like to say the number names.

❷ **Make up new verses for the counting rhyme.**
Ask children to draw five objects to say a rhyme about. Suggest different items for each child, for example: 'children sitting eating pie'; 'sports cars going for a ride'; 'bags of sweets, which one shall I buy?' etc. Once children have drawn their pictures, say the new rhymes, encouraging each child to point as you count.

Feedback

Can each child:
‣ say the numbers one to five correctly in order?
‣ point to each object correctly as they count?

Was any child too shy to join in?

Who was sufficiently confident to say alone the rhyme about their drawing?

2 Counting

Objective

Recite number names in order from one up to five.

Resources

▸ hand puppet, toy or cut-out face

What children are learning

to say the number names in order from one to five, sometimes slowly, sometimes more quickly

Words you can use

count, number, one, two, three, four, five

Things to note

▸ Children are not expected to be able to count five objects at this stage. Learning the sound and rhythm of the number names in order is one of the first steps towards counting.
▸ Controlling and varying the speed at which a child says the number names is also important in helping them to move beyond just saying them as a rhyme. Children have to adjust the speed they say number names when they begin to count objects and sounds.
▸ Children make a variety of common mistakes when counting such as saying words in the wrong order (one, two, three, five, four); missing a word out (one, three, four, five); repeating a word (one, two, two, four, five).

Activities

❶ **Count to five at different speeds.**
   ▸ Ask children to count together with you from one to five. Point to five children or objects as you count.
   ▸ Introduce the hand puppet and explain that it is going to show the children when to count. Scrunch the puppet up so that its face is hidden or down on the table (or hide the cut-out face behind a table). Open the puppet out (or make the face appear from behind the table) and say *One*.

Hide the puppet's face and wait. Encourage the children to look for signs that the puppet might come out again. Open the puppet out again and say *Two*. Continue this for three, four and five. Each time ensure that the children wait until they see the puppet's face before saying the next number.

▸ Begin counting again from one to five but vary the speed at which the puppet shows its face. Try counting quite quickly in this way, or very slowly, or a mixture of the two.

▸ Ask individual children to count as they see the puppet's face. Encourage each child to count as far as they can. Some children may be able to continue beyond five. For those who experience difficulty, show the puppet's face at a steady rate and allow them time to think.

❷ **Counting mistakes.**

The puppet can begin to 'talk'. Explain that it is going to count, but might sometimes make a mistake. Ask children to tell you if they hear a mistake. Count at varying speeds, sometimes making errors such as saying words in the wrong order *(One, two, three, five, four!)*; missing out a word *(One, three, four, five!)*; repeating a word *(One, two, two, four, five!* or *One, two, three, four, three!)*. Each time, ask children to say what was wrong and to count to five correctly.

Feedback

Can each child:

▸ say the numbers one to five correctly in order at varying speeds?
▸ recognize when a counting mistake has been made?

Did any child need prompting?

Which children could count beyond five? Could anyone count beyond ten?

3 Counting

Objective

Say and use number names to ten in order in familiar contexts, for example number rhymes, songs, stories.

Resources

▸ a number line on the wall could be used

What children are learning

familiarity with the rhythm and sound of the number names in order from one to ten

Words you can use

count, number, one, two, three, four, five, six, seven, eight, nine, ten

Things to note

▸ Children need plenty of opportunity to hear and recite the number names in order. Saying the rhymes together can help children who lack confidence.
▸ Any number rhymes, songs or stories can be used for this lesson. Choose any that children enjoy and are familiar with within the number range 1–10. Titles of further number rhymes and stories can be found on the NNS CD-ROM (sent to schools during spring 2000).
▸ Children are not expected to be able to count ten objects at this stage.

Activities

❶ **Action rhyme with numbers to ten.**
   ▸ Recite a rhyme which has the numbers one to ten in order and invite children to join in with the actions. Point to the numbers on a number line as you say the rhyme.

   The Tidying Rhyme
   One, two, so much to do,
   Three, four, let's sweep the floor,
   Five, six, pick up those bricks,
   Seven, eight, wash up that plate,
   Nine, ten, let's count again!

▸ Repeat the rhyme several times, each time putting your finger on your lips instead of saying a number name, beginning at one: *xxx, two, so much to do, three, four* … The next time miss out two numbers: *xxx, xxx, so much to do, three, four* … On the tenth time every number name is replaced: *xxx, xxx, so much to do, xxx, xxx, let's sweep the floor* … Encourage children to 'think' the missing number names in their heads.

❷ Counting story with numbers to ten.
Tell a 'numbers to ten' story, based on the idea below. Ask children to predict the number coming next in the story.

Sticky shoes
Once there was a boy called Ricky, who liked to walk everywhere. He walked to the park, he walked to the shops, he walked to the swimming pool. He would never go in his buggy. One day Ricky wore his best shoes. He walked into the kitchen and trod on some treacle and then everything began to go wrong. He had sticky shoes!
He walked into the street and **one** *paper bag got stuck on his sticky shoes.*
He walked to the park and **two** *crisp packets got stuck on his sticky shoes.*
He walked to the shops and **three** *sweet wrappers got stuck on his sticky shoes.*
He walked to the sweet shop and **four** *fruit pastilles got stuck on his sticky shoes* …
Encourage children to make up the rest of the story with you.

Feedback

Does each child know the number names from one to ten?

Which children were confident about which number came next in a rhyme or story?

Which children needed support/prompting?

4 Counting

Objectives

Recite number names in order from one up to ten.
Count reliably up to three objects.

Resources

▸ **PCM 1**
▸ three cards marked 'one', 'two', 'three'
▸ counters

What children are learning

▸ to say the number names in order from one to ten, sometimes slowly, sometimes more quickly
▸ to count up to three objects by pointing to each and saying the number names, or by looking at them and 'knowing' how many there are

Words you can use

count, number, one, two … ten

Things to note

▸ Some children find it difficult to point to objects one at a time as the number names are said. Count slowly and guide their finger if necessary. This action is known as *matching* or *one-to-one correspondence*, where one name is matched to one object.
▸ Children also need to realize that the number they say as they point to the last object tells them how many items there are in the group. Eventually they will learn to recognize two or three objects without needing to count them.
▸ Learning the sound and rhythm of the number names in order is one of the first steps towards counting. Controlling and varying the speed at which a child says the number names is also important in helping them to move beyond just saying the numbers as a rhyme. Children have to adjust the speed at which they say number names when they begin to count objects or sounds.
▸ Children make a variety of common mistakes when counting such as saying words in the wrong order (six, seven, nine, eight, ten); missing out a word (six, seven, nine, ten); repeating a word (six, eight, eight, nine, ten).

Activities

❶ Count to ten.

> ▸ Begin by practising counting together from one to ten. Use a rhyme such as *I've got walking fingers, looking for some fun, count along with them as they start to run … one, two …* 'Walk' your fingers across the table, varying the speed of each step; encourage children to count with you.

The river gameboard

> ▸ **The river game:** show children the gameboard on **PCM 1** and lay the three cards face down on the table. Explain that they are going to take turns. The game involves collecting counters from a pile and putting them on the stepping stones to reach the castle. Each child must count to ten to start their go. (Help those who find this difficult.) The child then picks a card from the three laid face down on the table. The card will show 'one', 'two' or 'three'. (Read the number if the child cannot.) The child then takes that many counters from a pile. Emphasize careful counting. The counters are placed on the stepping stones, starting at one side of the river. The next player then counts to ten, picks a card and adds their counters to those on the trail, working their way from the jetty across to the castle. The winner is the player who puts a counter on the last stepping stone to reach the castle.
>
> ▸ *Variations: cards marked 'four' and 'five' can be introduced if children can reliably count beyond three. The number of counters placed on the stepping stones can be counted after the first few turns.*

Feedback

Can each child:
▸ say the numbers one to ten correctly in order?
▸ count reliably three objects (or beyond)?

Did anyone find it difficult to match one number to one object when counting?

Did anyone think ahead and predict who might win the game?

5 Counting

Objective

Count reliably up to five objects.

Resources

▸ interlocking cubes
▸ picture cards or objects such as conkers or buttons

What children are learning

to count up to five objects by pointing to each and saying the number names, or by looking at them and 'knowing' how many there are; sometimes the arrangement of the items can help them 'know', as in the arrangement of dots on a dice, for example

Words you can use

count, number, one, two, three, four, five, how many?

Things to note

▸ Some children find it difficult to point to objects one at a time as the number names are said. Count slowly and guide their finger if necessary. This action is known as *matching* or *one-to-one correspondence*, where one name is matched to one object.
▸ Children also need to realize that the number they say as they point to the last object tells them how many items there are in the group. Eventually they will learn to recognize three, four or five objects without needing to count them.
▸ Children do not need to be able to write the numbers at this stage.

Activities

❶ Count five things.

▸ Count around the table *One, two …* pointing to each child in turn. Ask the children to repeat the count in unison. Count round the table with each child saying their number only. Repeat, starting with a different child.
▸ Lay out five objects (such as buttons or conkers) or picture cards in a line on the table. Count them in the same way. *How many buttons are there? One, two … How many conkers?* Rearrange the sets of objects and ask individual children to count them again.

❷ Make towers of cubes.

Ask children to count out two, three, four or five interlocking cubes and make them into a tower. Ensure children count the cubes one at a time and move them into a separate pile as they count to avoid confusion. Children can make several different towers, each from a different number of cubes. Compare the heights of different towers and ask questions about them. *Which is the largest tower? How many cubes is it made from? Look at this tower. Is it made from three or four cubes? Which is the smallest tower?* (made from two cubes) *Could we make an even smaller one?*

❸ Sort and count cubes.

Put about ten cubes in a selection of colours in a pile in the middle of the table. Ask a child to collect all the red cubes from the pile. This requires the child to sort the set of cubes and put them into some kind of order to count them. *How many are there?* Repeat for other colours in the pile, asking a different child each time. Encourage children to count carefully and for the others to agree whether they have counted correctly.

Feedback

Can each child count reliably five objects (or beyond)?

Did anyone recognize small quantities on sight (e.g. taking three cubes without counting)?

Did anyone need help?

6 Counting

Objective

Begin to recognize none and zero in stories and rhymes.

Resources

▸ finger puppets

What children are learning

▸ to use the words none and zero
▸ to begin to think of zero as a number that comes before one

Words you can use

count, number, zero, none, one, two … ten, how many?

Things to note

▸ Children sometimes find the concept of zero quite difficult as the early numbers they encounter are related to objects that they can see. The idea that zero is a number that comes before one can be confusing.

Activities

❶ **Count children sitting and standing.**
Ask the group to stand up. *How many children are standing?* Invite a child to count as you point to each child. Ask the girls to sit down. *How many are sitting? How many are standing?* Invite a child to count. Then ask children with brown hair to stand and the rest to sit. Continue to choose children to count the number that are sitting and standing. Repeat for other features, for example *Stand up if you have a sister/a dog/blue eyes/if you like chocolate/if you are five years old* etc.

❷ **Introduce zero.**
▸ Choose a feature that applies to all the children and ask them to stand, for example *Stand up if you are under seven years old. How many children are standing?* Invite a child to count everyone. Now ask how many are sitting. Explain that we call this number 'zero' or 'none'. *The number of people sitting is zero.*
▸ Choose other features that apply to all or none of the children and encourage children to answer using the words 'zero' or 'none'.

❸ **Finger puppets.**

Put a finger puppet on each finger of one hand.
Using the edge of the table, show the children
some of the puppets. Use the following rhyme:

*Five tall people standing in a row. Count them
very carefully.*
Now one of them has to go! (lower one finger)
Four tall people …
… One tall person standing all alone.
He has got to go now. Now there are none!

Finish by counting together backwards from five
to zero.

Feedback

Can each child use the word 'zero' or 'none' correctly?

Did anyone already know the meaning of 0?

Was that person able to explain the meaning of 0 to the others?

7 Adding (one more)

Objective
Find one more than (up to five objects).

Resources
▸ 0–10 number line
▸ objects for counting such as plastic farm animals, conkers or cubes
▸ 'number bears' made from **PCM 2**

What children are learning
to find (and eventually just say) the number that is one more than a number to 5

Words you can use
count, number, one, two, three, four, five, six, how many?, more, count on, one more

Things to note
▸ Children learn to say number names in order as a pattern of words. Once this is mastered, they need to begin to appreciate that, when counting forwards, a number they say is one more than the previous number, for example when counting forwards, four is one more than three, or that one more than five is six etc.
▸ Children may still need to count objects to be convinced of this fact so provide suitable objects such as plastic farm animals, conkers or cubes.

Activities
❶ **Find the number that is one more than a number up to five.**
  ▸ Show children a 0–10 number line. Ask them to count aloud from zero to ten. Pick individual numbers, for example 3 or 6. *What number is this?* Some children may not be confident with recognizing figures at this stage. Help them by giving the number name where necessary.
  ▸ Point to a number between 0 and 5, for example 4. *What number is this? Can you count out four animals/conkers/cubes for me?* Ask each child to take four objects from a central pile. Once each child has a set of four objects ask them to add one more to their set. *How many do you have now? Did anyone find the answer without counting their objects?* Encourage children to notice that five is the number that comes after four, so when adding one more we just count on one more.

- *What number is one more than four? Where is it on the number line?* Point to the numbers on the number line and emphasize that one more means we are 'counting on one'. *What number is one more than three? One more than five?* Repeat for all the numbers between 0 and 5.
- Use the 'number bears' on **PCM 2**. Show a number of bears between one and five. Ask children to count the number of bears and to say how many there would be if there was one more each time. *Four and one more is five.* Repeat for other numbers to 5.

  Variations: children could be shown a greater number of bears, for example up to nine, and could use the number line or their knowledge of the number names in order to find one more. Ask children to take turns to ask each other 'What number is one more than …?' and to say whether the answer is correct. This enables children to use the 'one more' vocabulary and to apply their understanding.

Feedback

Can each child say the number that is one more than a number to 5?

Who confidently recognized figures 0–10?

Who needed to count the set of objects again to respond to 'one more' questions?

Counting

Objective

Say and use number names to ten in order in familiar contexts, for example number rhymes, songs, stories.

Resources

▸ 'number bears' made from **PCM 2**

What children are learning

to say and use number names to ten in order in number rhymes, songs and stories etc.

Words you can use

count, number, one, two … ten, how many?

Things to note

▸ Children need plenty of opportunity to hear and recite the number names in order. Saying the rhymes together can help children who lack confidence.

▸ Any number rhymes, songs or stories can be used for this lesson. Choose any that children enjoy and are familiar with within the number range 1–10.

▸ The 'number bears' on **PCM 2** can be folded in different ways to show each of the numbers between one and ten. For example, in the picture the bottom row has been folded back to leave only six bears showing.

Activities

❶ **Say and use number names to ten in order.**

▸ Use the 'number bears' for this activity. Begin by folding so that only one bear can be seen. Say this rhyme, encouraging children to join in:

One little teddy bear sitting here today,
Along comes another friend who wants to stay and play.

Show two bears to the children. *How many bears are there now?*

> *Two little teddy bears sitting here today,*
> *Along comes another friend who wants to stay*
> *and play.*

Continue the rhyme, showing one more bear each time and asking children to say how many there are. *How do you know?* Continue until all ten bears are shown.

> *Ten little teddy bears sitting here today,*
> *It's getting late, it's time to go. They've had a lovely day.*

▸ Say another rhyme and ask children to join in with the actions such as:

> *One little **finger**, pointing to the sky, now I'm going to count it, will you have a try? One!*
> *Two little **fingers**, pointing to the sky, now I'm going to count them, will you have a try? One, two!*
> *Three little **fingers**, pointing to the sky, now I'm going to count them, will you have a try? One, two, three*

etc. up to ten.

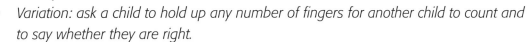 *Variation: ask a child to hold up any number of fingers for another child to count and to say whether they are right.*

Feedback

Can each child say the number names in order to ten?

Did anyone need encouragement to join in?

When a child called out the new number of bears, could they explain how they knew?

9 Comparing and ordering numbers

Objective

Recite number names in order from one up to twenty.

Resources

▸ hand puppet or toy

What children are learning

to say the number names in order from one to twenty, sometimes slowly, sometimes more quickly

Words you can use

count, count up to, number, one … ten, eleven … twenty, how many?

Things to note

▸ Children are not expected to be able to count twenty objects at this stage. It is important that they begin to recognize and repeat the sound and rhythm of the number names in order. Controlling and varying the speed at which a child says the number names is also important in helping them to move beyond just saying the numbers as a rhyme. Children have to adjust the speed at which they say number names when they begin to count objects and sounds.

▸ Children make a variety of common mistakes when counting such as saying words in the wrong order (six, seven, nine, eight, ten); missing out a word (six, seven, nine, ten); repeating a word (six, eight, eight, nine, ten).

▸ As children become more familiar with the numbers, ask them to listen for counting errors, spoken perhaps by a puppet, for example 'threeteen', fourteen, 'fiveteen', sixteen, seventeen, eighteen, nineteen, 'tenteen' etc.

▸ Make sure that children say thirteen, fourteen etc. clearly. When they speed up they tend to say thirty, forty etc., which causes confusion.

Activities

❶ **Count to ten.**

Begin with counting together from one to ten. Use a rhyme such as *I've got walking fingers, looking for some fun, count along with them as they start to run. One, two* … 'Walk' your fingers across the table, varying the speed of each step; encourage children to count with you.

❷ **Count to twenty at different speeds.**

▸ Introduce the hand puppet (or toy) and explain that it is going to show the children when to count. Scrunch the puppet up so that its face is hidden or on the table. Open the puppet out and say *One*. Hide the puppet's face and wait. Encourage the children to look for signs that the puppet might come out again. Open the puppet out again and say *Two*. Continue this for three, four etc. up to twenty, ensuring that the children wait until they see the puppet's face before saying the next number.

▸ Count again and vary the speed at which the puppet shows its face. Try counting quite quickly in this way, or very slowly, or a mixture of the two. Ask individual children to count as they see the puppet's face. Encourage each child to count as far as they can. Some children may be able to continue beyond twenty. For those who experience difficulty, show the puppet's face at a steady rate and allow them time to think.

▸ *Variation: let the children take turns to hold puppet and show/hide the face while the others count.*

Feedback

Can each child:

▸ say the numbers one to twenty correctly in order at varying speeds?
▸ recognize when a counting mistake has been made?

Did anyone wait to be prompted?

Could anyone count beyond twenty?

10 Comparing and ordering numbers

Objective

Use language such as *more* and *less, greater* or *smaller* to compare two numbers up to 5 and say which is more or less.

Resources

- several sets of 1–5 number cards
- raisins or similar small objects
- two saucers, yogurt pots or jar lids for each child

What children are learning

- to appreciate the relative sizes of numbers to 5
- to say which of two numbers is more or less/greater or smaller

Words you can use

count, count up to, number, one, two, three, four, five, how many?, the same, more, less, fewer, compare, greater, smaller

Things to note

- The words 'less' and 'fewer' are frequently used incorrectly. We use 'fewer' when comparing a number of objects (i.e. things that can be counted) as in fewer apples, buttons, items. 'Less' is used when we are comparing amounts or quantities (i.e. things that cannot be counted): there is less water, less sand, less time. Some supermarkets incorrectly use signs reading 'Less than 10 items', when the correct word is fewer. When describing a number generally (not a number of objects) we use 'less', for example less than 5. It is not vital that children are correct in this matter, but where possible, try to use the words appropriately.

Activities

❶ **Compare two sets of objects, saying which is more or less.**
- Provide each child with two saucers, yogurt pots or jar lids. Place different numbers of raisins (or similar) in each child's saucers, for example two in one, three in another. Ask children to count the number of raisins in each saucer. *How many raisins in this saucer?* Then ask children to say which container has more. *Which saucer has more raisins? Which has fewer raisins?* Then add some more raisins to the children's saucers and ask them to count both again, and compare them saying which has more raisins or which has fewer.

- Shuffle together several sets of 1–5 number cards and give one card to each child. Ask a child to place their card in the middle of the table and to say the number aloud. Help those who are unfamiliar with the figures. The next child lays their card next to the first card and says something about their card in relation to it, for example *My number is one; it is less than four; mine is the same as the last card.* Or *My number is four. It is more than two.* The next child places their card on top of the first card, so that only two cards can be seen and the game continues. Ask further questions, introducing the words greater than or smaller than, for example *Is this number greater than this number? Which is smaller? Are they both the same number?*

▶ *Variation: children could play this game in pairs, turning over cards from their own pile and making a statement comparing the two numbers.*

Feedback

Can each child:

- say which is more or less for two numbers up to 5?
- use language such as more and less, greater and smaller?

Who needed help/prompting to make a statement about the number cards?

Did anyone try to help or prompt an uncertain player?

Counting

Objective

Recite number names in order from one to twenty and beyond.

Resources

- 1–20 number track
- counters
- number dice

What children are learning

to say the number names in order from zero to twenty, sometimes slowly, sometimes more quickly

Words you can use

number, counting, zero, one, two … twenty, largest, smallest

Things to note

- The number names beyond ten do not follow a simple pattern. Children need to begin to recognize that not all the 'teen' numbers are made in the same way. Fourteen, sixteen, seventeen, eighteen and nineteen are the single numbers four, six, seven, eight and nine followed with 'teen'. Unfortunately thirteen and fifteen are not 'threeteen' and 'fiveteen'!
- As children become more familiar with the numbers ask them to listen for counting errors, spoken perhaps by a hand puppet, for example fourteen, 'fiveteen', sixteen, seventeen …
- Following eighteen and nineteen children may say 'tenteen' instead of twenty.
- Make sure that children say thirteen, fourteen etc. clearly, and do not shorten them to thirty, forty etc.

Activities

❶ **Say number names to twenty.**
- Invite the group to say in unison the numbers in order to twenty. Introduce a rhythm by clapping to maintain the pace of the count. Say the number names to twenty again but this time children say the next number when the count reaches them. When twenty is reached, ask the next child to begin again at zero. Vary the speed at which children say the number names by altering the beat. Ask individual children to count as far as they can.
- Call out some numbers in order and ask children to continue the count.

❷ Use a number track.

Introduce a 1–20 number track.

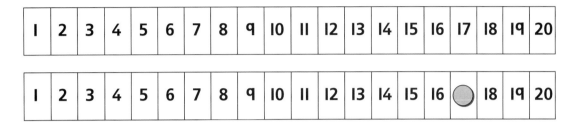

What do we use this for? What is it called? Which is the largest number on the track? Which is the smallest? Where would zero be? (Discuss that 0 comes before 1.) Count in unison to twenty, asking a child to touch each number on the track as it is spoken. Ensure that children recognize figures to 20 by inviting them to touch particular numbers on the track. *Who can touch seventeen?* etc. Cover up a number on the track. *Which number has been covered? How do you know?*

❸ Number track game.

Give each child a counter of a different colour. Take turns to roll a number dice and move forward along the number track. The winner is the first to reach 20. Ensure children say aloud the numbers that they roll and land on.

Feedback

Can each child say the number names in order to twenty?

Does anyone have difficulty recognizing figures between 10 and 20?

Who can continue counting beyond twenty?

12 Counting

Objective

Count reliably more than five objects.

Resources

- copy of **PCM 3** for each child
- coloured pencils
- counters

What children are learning

- to count more than five objects accurately
- to begin to recognize two, three or four items without needing to count them
- to draw more than five items

Words you can use

one, two … ten; number, count, how many?, more, less

Things to note

- Some children find it difficult to point to objects one at a time as the number names are said. Count slowly and guide their finger if necessary. This action is known as *matching* or *one-to-one correspondence*, where one name is matched to one object.
- Children also need to realize that the number they say as they point to the last object tells them how many items there are in the group. Eventually they will learn to recognize three, four, five or more objects without needing to point to them.
- Children do not need to be able to write the numbers at this stage.

Activities

❶ **Count items in a picture.**

- Give each child a copy of **PCM 3**. Discuss the picture. *What can you see? How many children are there? What do you think they are called? What are they doing? Who can see a balloon? How many balloons are there?* (5) *Who can see a frog? How many frogs are there?* (3) Note that the picture shows: one tree, two children, three frogs, four wellington boots, five balloons, six butterflies, seven birds, eight flowers, nine sheep and ten leaves.

- Beginning with the smaller numbers of items, encourage children to count each set carefully, pointing as they count. Counters or cubes could be placed on the items as they are counted to avoid confusion. Some children may be able to 'see', without counting, that there are two children, three frogs or four wellington boots.
- Ask the children to colour some of the items in the picture. *What colour are your wellington boots? Who has a green frog? How many frogs have you coloured?* For certain items in the picture ask children to colour only five of them. *Colour in five leaves, five flowers* etc. Once these are coloured, ask how many of each item are not coloured. *How many flowers have you left white?* (3) *How many butterflies are white?* (1) *Point to four white sheep, two white birds* etc.

❷ **Draw a numbers picture.**
As an additional activity, children could draw their own picture with one, two, three, four, five … ponds/fish/animals/people/trees/cars etc.

Feedback
Can each child:
- count reliably more than five objects?
- recognize two, three or four items without counting them?
- draw up to and more than five items accurately?

Do any of the children talk to themselves while colouring? ('I've done two boots, I've got two more to do.')

Note any conversations that show understanding of numbers.

13 Adding and subtracting (one more, one less)

Objective
Find *one more* or *one less* than a number up to 9.

Resources
- 0–10 number line
- objects for counting such as plastic farm animals, conkers or cubes
- 'number bears' made from **PCM 2**
- copy of **PCM 3** for each child

What children are learning
to find (and eventually just say) the number that is one more or one less than a number to 9

Words you can use
count, number, one, two … ten; how many? more, count on, one more, one less, fewer

Things to note
- Children learn to say number names in order as a pattern of words. Once this is mastered, they need to begin to appreciate that, when counting forwards, a number they say is one more than the previous number. For example, when counting forwards, four is one more than three, one more than five is six and so on. Similarly, when counting backwards, the next number is one less then the previous number.
- Children may still need to count objects to be convinced of this fact so provide suitable objects such as plastic farm animals, conkers or cubes.

Activities
❶ **Find the number that is one more than a number up to 9.**
Show children a 0–10 number line. Ask them to count aloud from 0 to 10. Pick individual numbers, for example 3 or 6. *What number is this?* Some children may not be confident with recognizing figures at this stage. Help them by giving the number name where necessary. *Can you count out six animals/conkers/cubes for me?* Once each child has made a set of six objects, ask them to add one more to their set. *How many do you have now? Did you know without counting your objects?* Encourage children to notice that seven is the number that comes after six, so when adding one more we just count on one more; demonstrate this on the number line. Ask further questions. *What number is one more than three? One more than five?* Repeat for all the numbers between 0 and 9.

❷ Find the number that is one less than a number up to 9.

▸ Give each child a copy of **PCM 3** and ask them to count the number of balloons, butterflies etc. *How many balloons are there?* (5) Tell them that one balloon has blown away and ask them to cross one off the picture. *How many balloons are left?* (4) *One less than five is four*. Repeat for other items in the picture, asking children to count them, cross one off and count again. Make the connection between 'one less' and counting backwards, showing them the numbers on the 0–10 number line.

▸ Use the 'number bears' on **PCM 2**. Show a number of bears between 1 and 9. Ask children to count the number of bears and say how many there would be if there was one fewer each time. Fold the bears to remove one bear. *How many bears are there now? One less than seven is six*. Repeat for other numbers to 9.

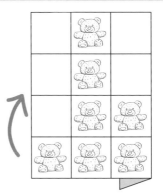

▸ Ask a child to fold the bears and ask a 'one more' or a 'one less' question.

Feedback

Can each child:
▸ say the number that is one more than a number to 9?
▸ say the number that is one less than a number to 9?

Does anyone need help in responding to 'one less' or 'one more' questions?

Who could answer 'one more' and 'one less' questions instantly without thinking?

14 Counting

Objective

Count reliably up to ten objects.

Resources

▸ 'number bears' made from **PCM 2**

What children are learning

▸ to count up to ten objects, eventually without needing to point
▸ to count objects that are arranged in a circle or are moving

Words you can use

zero, one, two … ten, counting, numbers, number names, how many?

Things to note

▸ Some children find it difficult to point to objects one at a time as the number names are said. Count slowly and guide their finger if necessary. This action is known as *matching* or *one-to-one correspondence*, where one name is matched to one object. Eventually children should be able to match the name to a number of objects without touching them.
▸ Children can be asked to put their hands behind their backs when counting a small number of objects; this encourages them to begin matching the number name with the objects without pointing. Eventually they will learn to recognize small numbers of objects without needing to count them.
▸ Objects arranged in a circle present a further counting problem. Children need to decide where to start counting and mark or make a note of this point. Similarly, for objects or items that are moving, such as fish in a tank or children in the playground, counting involves trying to keep a mental note of which items have already been counted.

Activities

❶ Count up to ten objects.

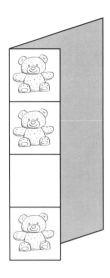

▸ Use 'number bears' copied from **PCM 2**. Fold over the sides so that children can see three bears. *How many bears can you see?* Invite a child to point to the bears and count them. Now fold the bears to show four or five bears. Ask children to guess how many there are before counting. *Are there more bears than last time?*

▸ Continue to fold the bears and encourage children to guess or to count without pointing; ask a child to check if they were right. Children could be introduced to the fact that there are ten bears altogether. *If you can see five bears, how many do you think I can see? If you can see nine bears, how many are hidden?* etc.

❷ Count up to ten objects arranged in a circle, or moving objects.

▸ Seat the children in a circle, or if there are fewer than five children arrange some toys or plastic animals in a circle. *Shall we count the children/objects?* Start counting around the circle but don't stop at the last child/object; keep counting. After a while ask the children how many there are. *Did I do something wrong? What did I do wrong?* Discuss that each child/object must be counted only once. Invite a child to count around the circle correctly, stopping at the correct place and stating the number of children/objects. If appropriate, ask another child to check.

▸ Now give each child between five and ten cubes and ask them to set them out in a circle. Then ask a child to count them carefully, remembering which object they started with, for example 'I started by counting the red one'.

▸ *Suppose I start somewhere else. Will the answer be the same? Are you sure?*

▸ Take the children for a walk around the classroom or school to count objects that are moving, for example fish in a fish tank or children outside or in a classroom. Alternatively ask some children to walk slowly around a small area and for the others to count them.

Feedback

Can each child:
▸ count up to ten objects reliably?
▸ count objects arranged in a circle?
▸ count moving objects?

Note which children devise their own strategy for counting moving objects or objects in a circle.

15 Counting

Objective

Count reliably up to ten objects or clapping sounds.

Resources

▸ copy of **PCM 3** for each child
▸ drum

What children are learning

▸ to count up to ten objects, eventually without pointing to them
▸ to count up to ten sounds

Words you can use

count, one, two … ten, number, number name, how many?

Things to note

▸ Some children find it difficult to point to objects one at a time as the number names are said. Count slowly and guide their finger if necessary. This action is known as *matching* or *one-to-one correspondence*, where one name is matched to one object. Eventually children should be able to match the name to an object without touching it.
▸ Children can be asked to put their hands behind their backs when counting a small number of objects; this encourages them to begin matching the number name with the objects without pointing.
▸ The counting of sounds and movements, which cannot be 'pointed to', is more difficult to master than counting objects.

Activities

❶ **Picture counting.**
  ▸ Give each child a copy of **PCM 3**. Discuss the picture. *What can you see? How many children are there?* (2) *What do you think they are called? What are they doing? Who can see a butterfly? How many butterflies are there?* (6) *Who can see a sheep? How many are there?* (9) Note that the picture shows: one tree, two children, three frogs, four wellington boots, five balloons, six butterflies, seven birds, eight flowers, nine sheep and ten leaves.

▸ Beginning with the smaller numbers of items, encourage children to count each set of items carefully, pointing as they count. Counters or cubes could be placed on the items as they are counted to avoid confusion. Some children may be able to 'see', without counting, that there are two children, three frogs or four wellington boots.

▸ Sing the following song about the five red balloons:
Five red balloons, sitting on the top, along comes a pin and then you hear a pop!
Four red balloons, sitting on the top, along comes a pin and then you hear a pop!
Three red balloons, sitting on the top, along …
Two red balloons, sitting on the top, along …
One red balloon, sitting on the top, along …
No red balloons, sitting on the top, just one little pin going pop, pop, pop, pop, pop!

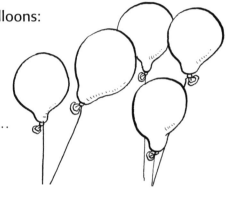

❷ **Count up to ten sounds.**
▸ Use a drum or clap several times. *How many balloons are being popped now?*
▸ Vary the volume of the sound each time, sometimes soft claps, sometimes loud and ask children to state how many they heard each time. Invite children to clap six times, make a 'pop' sound eight times, make a 'click' sound nine times etc.
▸ Ask a child to clap or make drum beats for others to count.

Feedback

Can each child:
▸ count up to ten objects?
▸ count up to ten sounds?

Which children can recognize small numbers without counting?

Does anyone have difficulty in counting sounds?

16 Money and 'real life' problems

Objectives

Recognize 1p coins.
Solve practical problems involving counting in 'real life' or role play.

Resources

- **PCM 1**
- four cards marked '1p', '2p', '3p', '4p'
- plenty of 1p coins

What children are learning

- to recognize 1p coins
- to understand that several of this coin are worth the same as 2p, 3p, 4p etc.

Words you can use

pence, total, add, plus, price, 1p, coins, penny

Things to note

- Children may already be familiar with money, but may need plenty of practice in making different totals with 1p coins.
- Real coins are preferred for this type of activity, although plastic coins are acceptable. If plastic coins are used, show a real 1p piece to the children to help them see how it differs from the plastic ones.
- Describe the 1p coin as '1p', 'one pence' and 'a penny' to widen children's vocabulary.

Activities

❶ **Collect 1p coins to make 1p, 2p, 3p, 4p.**

▸ Show children the gameboard on **PCM 1** and
set the four cards ('1p', '2p', '3p' and '4p') face
down in the middle of the table. The game
involves collecting 1p coins from a pile and
putting them on the stepping stones to reach
the castle. Each child must count to ten to
start their go. (Help those who find this
difficult.) The child can then pick a card from
the four on the table. The card will show '1p',
'2p', '3p' or '4p'. Ask children to say what the
card says (1p, 2p, 3p or 4p). The child then
collects the amount from the pile of 1p coins.
Emphasize careful counting. The coins should
be placed on the stepping stones, starting at
one side of the river. The next player then counts to ten, picks a card and adds
their coins to those on the trail, working their way from the jetty across to the
castle. The winner is the first player to put a coin on the last stepping stone.

The river gameboard

▸ Ask the children to count the coins with you as far as they can. Count all the 1ps.

▸ *Variation: cards marked '5p' and '6p' can be introduced if appropriate.*

Feedback

Can each child:

▸ recognize 1p coins?

▸ make amounts such as 2p, 3p, 4p etc. using 1p coins?

Did anyone think ahead and predict who might win the game?

Did anyone need help when counting to ten?

Objective

Say and use number names beyond ten in order in familiar contexts, for example number rhymes, songs, stories.

Resources

▸ a hand puppet or toy

What children are learning

familiarity with the rhythm and sound of the number names in order to ten and beyond

Words you can use

number, counting, zero, one, two … twenty, before, after, next, count on

Things to note

▸ The number names beyond ten do not follow a simple pattern. Children need to begin to recognize that not all the 'teen' numbers are made in the same way. Fourteen, sixteen, seventeen, eighteen and nineteen are the single numbers four, six, seven, eight and nine followed with 'teen'. Unfortunately thirteen and fifteen are not 'threeteen' and 'fiveteen'!

▸ Following eighteen and nineteen children may use the word 'tenteen' instead of 'twenty'. Children also make the mistake of confusing the numbers 12 and 20, as both start with a 'twe' sound and have the digit 2.

▸ Make sure children say teen numbers clearly and do not shorten the words to thirty, forty etc.

Activities

❶ **Say number names up to and beyond ten in order.**

▸ Begin by saying the action rhyme *One potato, two potatoes, three potatoes, four …;* children join in by placing fists on top of each other as the rhyme is spoken. Continue until the number range is too difficult for the children.

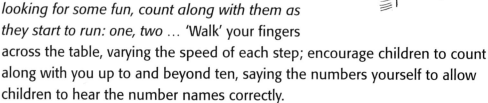

▸ Use a rhyme such as *I've got walking fingers, looking for some fun, count along with them as they start to run: one, two …* 'Walk' your fingers across the table, varying the speed of each step; encourage children to count along with you up to and beyond ten, saying the numbers yourself to allow children to hear the number names correctly.

❷ Listen for counting errors.
- ▸ Introduce the hand puppet (or toy) and explain that it is going to do some counting but that it might make a mistake. Tell the children that you want them to place their hands on their heads if they hear a mistake. Begin counting from zero, one or another small number and count beyond ten, making errors, for example:

  … six, seven, eight, nine, eleven …
  … eight, nine, ten, eleven, twenty …
  … nine, ten, eleven, twelve, 'threeteen' …

- ▸ Discuss the errors made. Ask the children to take turns with the puppet, saying the number names in order as far as they can. If a mistake is made, it can be the puppet at fault!

Feedback

Can each child say and use number names in order up to and beyond ten?

When a child has the hand puppet, note how far they can count without making a mistake.

18 Counting

Objective
Recite number names in order, continuing from two, three or four.

Resources
▸ drum
▸ 1–20 number cards

What children are learning
to continue a number count starting from a small number, for example three or four

Words you can use
number, counting, zero, one, two … twenty, before, after, next, count on

Things to note
▸ Children of a young age learn to recognize and recite the numbers in order, beginning first at one, then at zero. To begin reciting the numbers starting at any small number is an extra step for them. This can affect the rhythm and pattern of words that children have learnt and can prove difficult for some.
▸ Children may find moving to a beat and counting at the same time more difficult than counting while sitting down. Their attention at first may be on the marching and listening to the beat rather than on counting. With practice, however, children become more confident with this activity.
▸ Controlling and varying the speed at which a child says the number names is also important in helping them to move beyond just saying the numbers as a rhyme. Children have to adjust the speed at which they say the number names when they begin to count objects and sounds.

Activities
❶ **Recite number names in order, continuing from a small number.**
   ▸ Ask some 'What comes next?' questions such as *One, two, three, what comes next? Two, three, four, what comes next? Three, four, five, what comes next?* and so on. If children are confident with saying their number names in order, the questions can include counting forwards from other numbers to ten, for example *Five, six, seven, what comes next?* or counting backwards, for example *Six, five four, what comes next?*

▸ Share out a set of 1–20 number cards (1–10 if more appropriate). Ask each child in turn to lay a card on the table and say the number aloud. Help children to place the cards in order (some may find this difficult) so that a 1–20 number track is spread across the table. Keeping the cards in the same positions, turn them face down, starting at one and counting along as you do so.

'… five, six, seven …'

Once the cards are face down, ask a child to turn over three consecutive cards. Invite children to say the three numbers. *Can you count on from here?* Reveal the cards to check. Repeat for other sequences, giving each child a turn at choosing the three start numbers.

▸ Take the children to an area where they can move around freely. Using a drum, tap a beat for the children to march to. As children are marching to the beat, call out a number as you hit the drum, for example *Three!* Children must keep marching but continue counting from the number *(Four, five, six …)* until you call *Stop!* Repeat for other small numbers. Vary the speed of the beat to make this activity more difficult.

Feedback

Can each child recite number names in order, continuing from two, three or four?

Does anyone have difficulty responding to instructions?

Does anyone in the group find this particularly easy?

19 Comparing and ordering numbers

Objective
Order a given set of numbers (for example, 1–6) given in random order.

Resources
▸ 1–6 number cards
▸ corresponding number name cards

What children are learning
to order the numbers 1–6 when given randomly

Words you can use
more, less, greater, smaller, number, one, two … six, count, order, number name

Things to note
▸ In order to arrange a set of numbers in order, children must first appreciate which of two numbers is greater and which is smaller.
▸ Children need to begin to recognize figures. If children cannot match the number name with the figure tell them what it is called. Number name cards can be placed in order if more appropriate for the children.
▸ Children could be provided with a number line or track to help them with these activities.

Activities
❶ **Compare two numbers, saying which is more or less.**
▸ Give out the 1–6 number cards so that each child has one card. Children should lay their cards in front of them so that everyone can see. Ask each child in turn to make a statement about their own number in comparison with another child's number, for example *My number is six. It is larger than Claire's card which is five. My number is four. It is one more than Tim's card which is three.*

19

- Ask questions about the cards: *Who has the smallest number? If we were to put you in order starting at one, who would be last? Whose card shows the number that comes after two?* etc. Encourage the children to stand in a line in order. Ordinal numbers such as first, second and third could be discussed at this point: *Who is third? Which number are you holding?*
- Give a number card to all children except one. Ask the child who does not have a card to place the other children in order in a line. Give each child a turn at being 'in charge' of the line.

❷ Order the numbers 1–6.

Shuffle a set of 1–6 number cards. Children take turns to pick a card from the set and place it on the table. *What number is it? Is it larger than two? Than five?* etc. As each new card is turned, encourage children to place it in order, rearranging the cards on the table where necessary.

▶ *Variations: include a wider range of numbers, for example 1–8 or 1–9, or ask children to order number cards from 4 to 10, etc.*

Feedback

Can each child:

- compare two numbers and say which is more or less?
- order the numbers 1 to 6 when given randomly?

Do children answer yes/no to questions such as *Is six more than four?* Can they phrase a statement of their own such as 'six is more than four'?

20 Counting

Objective

Count reliably up to twelve objects.

Resources

▸ 0–12 number cards
▸ dominoes (with spots)
▸ copy of **PCM 4** for each child

What children are learning

▸ to count accurately up to twelve objects
▸ to draw sets of up to twelve objects

Words you can use

zero, one, two … twelve, more, less, greater, smaller, number, count

Things to note

▸ Call the 0-card 'zero'. The word 'none' could also be used to describe the number of spots on the 0,0 domino.
▸ Some children find it difficult to point to objects one at a time as the number names are said. Count slowly and guide their finger if necessary. This action is known as *matching* or *one-to-one correspondence*, where one name is matched to one object.

Activities

❶ **Count up to twelve objects using dominoes.**

▸ Lay out the 0–12 number cards in a line along the table. Place a set of dominoes face down. Ask each child to pick a domino and to count the number of spots on the domino. *Which of these dominoes has the most spots?* Encourage each child to find the number card with the matching figure (for example, 7). Children may not recognize the figure yet so help them to find it and remind them how to say the number (for example, seven).

▸ Invite each child to place their domino by the matching number card. Continue in the same way, ensuring that children are counting correctly. If children struggle to count accurately, draw the arrangement of spots on paper in a larger form and invite the child to point or place a counter on each spot as they count.

20

▸ Once the dominoes have been sorted, ask further questions: *How many spots do these dominoes have? Can you point to a domino with seven spots? How many dominoes have four spots?* etc.

❷ **Draw sets of twelve objects.**
Ask children to draw spots on the dominoes on **PCM 4** so that all the dominoes have twelve spots. Spots can be arranged in different ways such as 6,6 or 11,1 and so on. Encourage children to count the number of spots carefully each time to check that there are twelve.

▶ *Variation: some children could be asked to draw dominoes with six, eight or ten spots if more appropriate for their counting skills.*

Feedback

Can each child:
▸ count reliably up to twelve objects?
▸ draw sets of twelve objects?

Did some children recognize dot patterns on sight and use them to count on?

Note any children who still make errors when counting. Is it because they do not make one-to-one correspondence between the number and the object, or because items to be counted are missed out?

Adding and subtracting

Objectives

Begin to use the language involved in adding.
Begin to relate addition to combining two groups of objects, counting all the objects.

Resources

▸ objects for counting such as pasta shells, cubes or toy cars
▸ a large hoop

What children are learning

to appreciate that 'adding' is when we combine two groups and find how many items we have in total

Words you can use

and, makes, add, plus, equals, altogether

Things to note

▸ Children do not need to read or write addition statements such as $3 + 4 = 7$ at this stage. It is important that they have plenty of experience of counting two separate groups of objects and putting the two groups together. The total of these two groups is then found.
▸ Use similar items to make the two sets. It is not appropriate for children of this age to be adding completely different sets of objects, for example 4 pigs and 2 counters is 6 'things'. Always make sure that the two groups of objects can be combined to make one set, for example 4 red cubes and 2 blue cubes is 6 cubes.

Activities

① Add 1, 2 or 3.

> ▸ Put a large hoop in the middle of the table. Place
> three similar items (three cubes, three pasta shells
> or three cars, for example) close together in one
> part of the hoop. *How many cubes are there in the
> hoop?* Ask a child to count them to check. Place
> another two cubes close together in a different part
> of the hoop. *How many cubes have I just put in the*

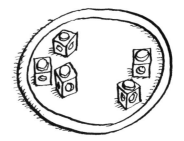

> *hoop?* Once children have counted the new set, ask *How many objects are in
> the hoop altogether?* Push the objects together and ask a child to count them.
> Describe this as *Three cubes and two more makes five cubes. Three and two
> makes five. Three add two is five.* Demonstrate by separating the objects into
> their original groups and putting them back together as you describe the process.
> Repeat for different start numbers (for example, four, two or five) and add one,
> two or three to each. Emphasize the numbers in each case: *Four cars and three
> cars is how many cars? So four add three is how many altogether?*
>
> ▸ Children work in pairs. Each child rolls a dice and collects that number of objects
> from the central pile. (For example, one rolls a 3 and the other a 4; they collect
> three and four objects, respectively.) They count each set and then combine the
> sets and count the total, creating an adding sentence: 4 cubes add 3 cubes
> equals 7 cubes; 4 add 3 equals 7.
>
> ▸ Pairs take turns to explain one of their addition sums to the rest of the group.

Feedback

Can each child:

> ▸ appreciate that adding is when two groups are combined?
> ▸ answer simple addition questions?

Could anyone add the two numbers without counting?

Did anyone have difficulty putting the addition into words?

Adding and subtracting

Objective

Separate (partition) a given number of objects into two groups.

Resources

- two saucers, yogurt pots or jar lids for each child
- raisins or similar small objects
- interlocking cubes

What children are learning

to begin to appreciate that a number of items can be split into two groups

Words you can use

count, split, number, how many?, one, two … twenty, partition, set, sort

Things to note

- This type of activity, in which one number is split into two parts, can help children to begin to appreciate early ideas of subtraction or division. It also can help them to make the link between addition and subtraction: once part of a set of objects is removed (subtraction), the two parts can be put back together again (addition).
- Avoid using the addition or equals sign when recording at this stage; instead use the words 'and' and 'equals'.

Activities

❶ **Split a set of objects into two groups.**
- Give each child two saucers (or yogurt pots or jar lids) and five raisins (or similar). *How many raisins have I given you?* Ask the children to place some raisins in each saucer, for example two in one and three in the other. Ask children to count the number of raisins in each saucer. *How many have you put in this saucer? How many in this one?* Discuss the different ways in which the children have partitioned the five raisins, for example four and one. If all have arranged them in the same way ask them to find a different way of arranging them. Describe this as: *Five can be split into three and two, five can be partitioned into four and one.* The ways of partitioning five can be recorded on a large piece of paper or on the board.

▸ Provide children with a different number of raisins, for example six or seven, and repeat the activity. Ask each child to make a stick of eight interlocking cubes. *How many cubes have you in your stick? Are you sure you have eight?* Ask them each to break their stick into two pieces and count the number of cubes in each part. Encourage them to describe this as, for example *'I have split eight into seven and one'*. Ask children to find different ways of splitting eight cubes into two parts. Again, these partitions can be recorded on paper.

▸ *Variation: sticks can be made from fewer or more cubes, as appropriate for the children.*

Feedback

Can each child separate (partition) a set of five, six, seven or eight objects into two groups?

Did anyone systematically find different ways of splitting eight cubes into two groups (i.e. 7,1; 6,2; 5,3; 4,4)?

Who found it hard to explain what they had done?

Objective

Recite the number names in order, counting back from six, five or four.

Resources

▸ 0–10 number cards

What children are learning

▸ to say the number names in order backwards from six, five or four
▸ to begin to count backwards a certain number of steps, for example count back three numbers from 5

Words you can use

number, counting, zero, one, two … ten, before, after, next, forwards, backwards

Things to note

▸ Counting backwards is a useful skill for helping children with subtraction. Initially children learn to recite the number names in order backwards from numbers up to 6. The next step is being able to count back a certain number of steps, for example count back three numbers from 5. This requires children to keep a check of how many numbers they have said. Children of this age will use their fingers to help them keep count.

Activities

❶ **Count backwards and say the next number.**
I am going to count backwards. Can you tell me which number comes next? Ask some 'what comes next?' questions starting from 4, 5 or 6: *Four, three, two, what comes next? Five, four, three, what comes next? Six, five, four, what comes next?* If children are confident with saying their number names in order, you could include some questions that involve counting backwards from other numbers to ten: *Seven, six, five, what comes next? Eight, seven, six, what comes next?*

❷ Count backwards from six to zero – Blast off!

‣ Ask children to crouch down by their chairs. Tell the children they are rockets waiting for 'blast off'. Begin the count at six and ask the children to join in: *Six, five, four, three* … On reaching zero the children shout 'Blast off' and jump into the air as if they are rockets taking off. Repeat several times if necessary. Ask individual children to say the countdown for everyone else to 'blast off'. If appropriate, start the countdown with a number beyond 6.

‣ Ask questions such as *What number is one smaller than six? Than four?* etc. Encourage children to use counting backwards one step as a way of finding out.

❸ Count backwards a certain number of steps.

‣ Hold up the 5-card and ask children to count back two steps, using their fingers to keep count. *Hold up two fingers. We are going to put the number five in our heads. Think the number five and now count back slowly.* As each new number is said, children should lower a finger. *Which number do we end on?* Repeat, asking children to count back three or four steps from 5.

‣ Hold up a different number card, for example the 6-card. Again, ask children to count back two, three or five steps from that number, using their fingers to help them.

‣ If you have a painted number line in the playground, ask children to take turns to stand on a given number then to step back one, two or three spaces. *What number do you land on? Eight count back three is five.*

Feedback

Can each child:
‣ say the number names in order backwards from 6, 5 and 4?
‣ count backwards a certain number of steps?

Did anyone need help counting back from 6?

When counting back a certain number of steps, did anyone predict the answer without counting back?

Objective

Count reliably up to twelve objects, claps or hops.

Resources

- gameboard from **PCM 5**, enlarged to A3 if possible
- counters or buttons for counting
- dice
- 1–12 number cards

What children are learning

- to count up to twelve objects with accuracy
- to count up to twelve sounds or movements

Words you can use

count, number, one, two … twelve, how many?, more, less

Things to note

- Some children find it difficult to point to objects one at a time as the number names are said. Count slowly and guide their finger if necessary. This action is known as *matching* or *one-to-one correspondence*, where one name is matched to one object. Eventually children should be able to match the name to an object without touching it.
- Children can be asked to put their hands behind their backs when counting a small number of objects; this encourages them to begin matching the number names to the objects without pointing. The counting of sounds and movements, which cannot be 'pointed to', is more complex.
- Help the children to read the figures; some children may not yet be confident with figures in this range.

Activities

❶ **Count up to twelve objects.**
Place a pile of counters or buttons on the table. Working in pairs, children take turns to collect a handful of counters from the pile. *How many counters in your handful?* The first child counts and announces the number. The second child then counts them as a check. If the first child was correct s/he takes a counter. The winner is the first to collect ten counters.

❷ Count up to twelve movements.

▸ If possible, move to an area where children can move around freely. Ask a child to stand slightly away from you and to walk towards you slowly. The rest of the children in the group should count the number of steps s/he takes. Choose a different child and a new starting point. Again, ask the group to count the number of steps taken to reach you. *Were more steps taken this time or last time?*

▸ Ask all the children to stand along a line, side by side, and to walk forward six, eight, eleven or twelve paces. Some children will have smaller paces than others. Count together as they take each step. Repeat for hops, asking children to hop seven, ten hops etc.

❸ Trail game.

Use the gameboard on **PCM 5** to play this game. Shuffle a set of 1–12 number cards and place them face down in a pile. Place a counter for each child on the start position. Children take turns to roll the dice and move forward that many squares. When they land on a square they pick a 1–12 number card and follow the instruction on the board, for example clap or blink, that many times. Ensure that the other children count carefully to check whether the child follows the instructions correctly.

▸ *Variation: shuffle a set of 1–12 number cards. Players take turns to pick up a card and ask the person on their right to do an action that many times, for example 'Peter, tap the table nine times'. Everyone checks, then Peter picks up a card and challenges the person to his right and so on.*

Feedback

Can each child:
▸ accurately count up to twelve objects?
▸ count up to twelve sounds or movements?

Did anyone count in their heads, instead of counting aloud?

Did anyone lose count and have to start again?

25 Adding and subtracting

Objectives

Begin to use the language involved in subtracting.
Relate subtraction to taking away, counting how many are left.

Resources

- cubes
- dice
- 'number bears' made from **PCM 2**

What children are learning

- that when we 'take away' we remove some of a set and see how many are left
- that this is called subtraction

Words you can use

subtract, take away, minus, how many?, number

Things to note

- There are two main types of subtraction, one is 'taking away' a number from another; the other is finding the difference between two numbers. Practically, these two types of question would be tackled in different ways. This lesson is helping children to understand subtraction as removing part of a number – 'taking away'.
- Children do not need to read or write subtraction statements such as $10 - 4 = 6$ at this stage. It is important that they have plenty of experience of removing a set of objects from another set and counting to see how many are left.

Activities

❶ **Use the vocabulary involved in subtraction.**
Play this game using cubes and a dice. Each child should begin with an equal number of cubes (about twenty). Children should count their cubes to check the number. The children take turns to roll the dice and take away that many cubes from their pile, placing them in a central pile on the table. As each child takes their turn, describe the situation using a range of vocabulary:

Jamie is taking away three!

Sandeep is subtracting four!

Ella has to take five!

The winner is the first child to have taken away all their cubes. As the game nears its conclusion, encourage children to count their remaining cubes and say which number they would need to roll to finish.

▶ *Variation: a dice marked 1, 1, 2, 2, 3, 3 could be used and fewer cubes given to each child to start, for example fourteen.*

❷ **Relate subtracting to taking away and counting how many are left.**
Show children the 'number bears' on **PCM 2**. *How many bears can you see?* (10)
Now fold over one side to hide one bear. *How many bears have I hidden? How many can you see now?* Ask children to count the remaining bears. *I started with ten bears. I have taken away one and there are nine left.* Show them the ten bears again and fold over the side with two bears. *How many bears have I hidden? How many are left?* Ask children to count the remaining bears. *I started with ten bears. I have taken away two and there are eight left.* Continue in this way for other numbers subtracted from ten.

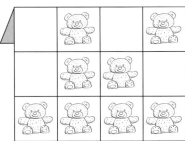

Feedback

Is each child beginning to understand subtraction as taking away?

Can each child count how many objects are left when some are taken away?

Who confidently used 'taking away' vocabulary to say what they were doing?

In activity 1, did anyone keep a check on how many cubes they had left each time?

Money and 'real life' problems

Objective
Sort coins: 1p, 2p, 5p.

Resources
▸ 1p, 2p and 5p coins
▸ feely bag
▸ 'money monsters' (toys or pictures labelled 1p, 2p and 5p)

What children are learning
▸ to recognize and name 1p, 2p and 5p coins
▸ to sort the coins into groups

Words you can use
sort, set, coins, 1p, 2p, 5p, pence, penny, how many?, count, number, more, fewer

Things to note
▸ Some children may already be familiar with money, but may require plenty of practice in making different totals with coins.
▸ Real coins are preferred for this type of activity, although plastic coins are acceptable. If plastic coins are used, show real coins to the children to help them see how these differ from the plastic ones.
▸ Describe the 1p coin as '1p', 'one pence' and 'a penny' to widen children's vocabulary.

Activities
❶ **Recognize 1p, 2p and 5p coins.**
Put several 1p, 2p and 5p coins into a feely bag. Children take turns to take a coin from the bag. The winner is the first child to collect two of each of the coins. They can arrange the coins in order of value, to emphasize that their value is not related to their actual size. Children can make rubbings of each coin and write its value alongside.

❷ Sort 1p, 2p and 5p coins – money monsters.
Place a mixture of 1p, 2p and 5p coins in a pile on the table. Ask a child to find a 1p coin. Ask questions about it: *What shape is it? Is it silver? How much is it worth?* Repeat for the other coins. Introduce the 'money monsters', which can be three pictures or soft toys labelled '1p', '2p' and '5p'. Explain that each monster can eat only one type of coin. Ask the children to sort out the pile of coins so that each monster gets the right coins to eat.

❸ Sort 1p, 2p and 5p coins – footprints.
▸ Ask children to draw around one of their feet three times on a piece of paper and to label the footprints '1p', '2p' and '5p'. (Hands could be used instead, if fingers are kept together.) Ask children to find how many of each coin will fit inside their footprint, for example 'I can fit twelve pennies into my footprint'; 'I can fit eight 2p coins into my footprint' etc.

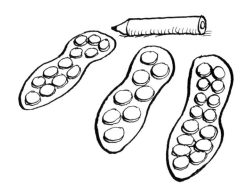

▸ Compare the different sizes of footprint by seeing whose foot was 'worth' the most/least using 1p coins, then using 2p coins etc. *How many 2p coins fitted into your footprint? Was this more or fewer than fitted into Jamie's footprint?*

Feedback

Can each child:
▸ recognize 1p, 2p and 5p coins?
▸ sort 1p, 2p and 5p coins?

When the children are ordering the coins can they say which is 'worth more than' or 'worth the same as' or 'has the same value as'?

Did anyone count in twos when finding out what their footprint was 'worth'?

27 Counting and reading numbers

Objective
Recognize figures 1 to 3.

Resources
▸ figures 1, 2 and 3 made from felt, sandpaper or plastic
▸ five cards of each of the figures 1 to 3
▸ gameboard from **PCM 1**, enlarged to A3 if possible
▸ counters

What children are learning
to recognize and name the figures 1–3

Words you can use
number, count, one, two, three, how many?

Things to note
▸ Children sometimes find it difficult to relate their understanding of numbers such as one, two and three to squiggles on a page. Feeling the shapes of the figures made from felt, sandpaper or other textures is useful.
▸ Discuss the different figures in terms of whether they are made from straight lines or curved lines or a combination of both.

Activities
❶ **Introduce figures 1–3.**
Show children the figures cut from felt or made from sandpaper and ask them to feel the numbers with their eyes closed. *Do you know which number this is?* Discuss whether the figures are made from curved or straight lines: 1 is made from a straight line, 3 is 'half a round' and 'half a round' on top of each other, 2 has a curved line and a straight line. If plastic figures are available, children can close their eyes and try to guess which number they are feeling.

27

❷ **Recognize figures 1–3.**
Give each child a number name: 'one', 'two' or 'three'. More than one child can have the same number. Tell them they must remember which number they are. *What was your number? And yours?* Shuffle the fifteen cards showing the figures 1 to 3 and place them face down in a pile. Children take turns to turn over a card from the pile. *What number is on your card?* If the figure matches their given number they can keep the card. If the figure is not the same as their number they return it to the bottom of the pile. Continue until all the cards have been given out.

❸ **Recognize figures 1–3 and count that many objects.**
Use the river gameboard from **PCM 1** and the 1–3 figure cards to play this game. Children take turns to pick a figure card from the pile. They collect that many counters and place them on the stepping stones across the river. Each child adds their counters to those on the trail, working their way from the jetty across to the castle. The winner is the player to place the last counter on a stone to reach the castle.
▷ *Variations: cards marked with the figures 4 and 5 can be introduced if children are comfortable with the figures 1 to 3. The number of counters placed on the stepping stones can be counted after the first few turns.*

Feedback

Can each child recognize figures 1 to 3?

Did any child repeatedly confuse figures 2 and 3?

When playing the river game, did any child pick up the right number of counters without counting?

28 Comparing and ordering numbers

Objectives

Compare two numbers.
Say a number that lies between two given numbers up to ten (then beyond).

Resources

▸ cubes
▸ several sets of 0–10 number cards
▸ 0–10 number track or number line

What children are learning

▸ to appreciate the relative sizes of numbers (which is vital if children are to be able to compare and order them)
▸ to learn to use the word 'between' in relation to two numbers

Words you can use

between, count, count up to, number, one ... five, how many?, the same, more, less, fewer, compare, greater, smaller

Things to note

▸ Use a number line to draw children's attention to numbers that lie between two other numbers, for example 5 lies between 3 and 9. During the activities, once a child has suggested one number that lies between two others, encourage children to suggest other numbers: *Which other numbers are between three and nine? What other numbers could s/he have said?* (4, 6, 7 or 8)
▸ The words 'less' and 'fewer' are frequently used incorrectly. We use 'fewer' when comparing a number of objects (i.e. things that can be counted) as in fewer apples, buttons, items. 'Less' is used when we are comparing amounts or quantities (i.e. things that cannot be counted): there is less water, less sand, less time. Some supermarkets incorrectly use signs reading 'Less than 10 items', when the correct word is 'fewer'. When describing a number generally (not a number of objects) we use 'less', for example less than 5. It is not vital that children are correct in this matter, but where possible, try to use the words appropriately.

28

Activities

❶ Compare two sets of objects and say which is more.

Ask each child to take a handful of cubes and to count them carefully. *How many cubes have you got?* Encourage children to compare sets of cubes. *Do you have more cubes than Ravi? Has Jenny fewer cubes than Peter? How many cubes have you got, Jack? Does anyone have more cubes than you?*

❷ Compare two numbers, say which is more or less and give a number in-between.

▸ Shuffle several sets of 0–10 number cards and place them face down in two equal piles. Children take turns to turn over the top card from each pile, for example 4 and 7. The child then says which is the larger number and which is smaller or whether both cards are the same. Ask them to explain each time: *Eight is more than seven. Four is more than three.* If correct, the child gets a counter. They can have an extra counter if they give a number that lies between the two numbers, where possible. Continue until all the cards have been used. If children find this difficult they can use a number line to help them. Alternatively the cards can be limited to 0–5 or 0–6.

▸ Give a 0–10 number card to each child. Ask a child to start by placing their card in the middle of the table and saying the number aloud. The next child lays their card next to the first card and says something about their card in relation to the previous card, for example *My number is eight; it is more than seven. Mine is the same as the last card. My number is three; it is less than eight.* The next child places their card on top of the first card, so that only two cards can be seen and the game continues. Ask further questions, introducing the phrases 'greater than' or 'smaller than': *Is this number greater than this number? Which is smaller? Are they both the same number?* Ask children, where possible, to name a number between the two numbers.

Feedback

Can each child:
▸ compare two numbers between 0 and 10 and say which is more or less?
▸ give a number that lies between two such numbers?

Who could make a confident statement about two numbers?

Who needed help and reassurance?

29 Counting and reading numbers

Objectives

Count reliably up to fifteen.
Recognize figures 1 to 5.
Recognize small numbers without counting.

Resources

- cubes
- counters or buttons for counting
- 1–5 number track

What children are learning

- to count up to fifteen objects, recognizing smaller numbers of them without counting
- to recognize the figures 1–5

Words you can use

number, counting, one, two … fifteen

Things to note

- Some children find it difficult to point to objects one at a time as the number names are said. Count slowly and guide their finger if necessary. This action is known as *matching* or *one-to-one correspondence*, where one name is matched to one object.

Activities

❶ **Count reliably up to fifteen objects.**
   Place a pile of counters or buttons on the table. Working in pairs, children take turns to collect a handful of counters from the pile. The first child counts the counters and announces the total. The second child then counts them as a check. If the first child was correct s/he takes a cube. The winner is the first to collect ten cubes. Depending on the size of the objects being used, children may need to take two handfuls as the game develops, to increase the numbers towards fifteen.

29

❷ Recognize small numbers without counting.
Ask the children to sit with their fists clenched and resting on the table. Invite a child to hold up one hand showing up to five fingers. As quickly as possible, the other children should say the number of fingers shown. The first child to do so correctly wins a counter or cube. The fingers should be counted each time as a check. Play continues around the group. Encourage children to respond quickly without counting, to help them to develop a sense of the numbers.

❸ Recognize figures 1 to 5.
Play the fingers game again. This time the first child to say the correct number wins a counter only if they can also point to it on a 1–5 number track.

▶ *Variation: if children find numbers to five too difficult, you can lead the activity by showing one, two or three fingers initially. When children are successful in this range, include four, and then five.*

Feedback

Can each child:
▸ count up to fifteen objects, recognizing smaller numbers without counting?
▸ recognize the figures 1–5?

Did anyone find it difficult to count accurately every time?

Notice how children count large numbers: are they quick and confident, or slow and painstaking?

30 Adding and subtracting

Objective

Relate addition to combining two, then three groups.

Resources

▸ objects for counting such as shells, cubes or toy frogs
▸ dice
▸ a large hoop

What children are learning

▸ to appreciate that 'adding' is when we combine groups and find how many items we have in total
▸ to appreciate that 'adding' can involve combining more than two numbers or groups

Words you can use

and, makes, add, plus, equals, altogether, total

Things to note

▸ Children do not need to read or write addition statements such as 3 + 4 = 7 at this stage. It is important that they have plenty of experience of counting two separate groups of objects and putting the two groups together. The total of these two groups is then found.
▸ Use similar items to make the two sets. It is not appropriate for children of this age to be adding completely different sets of objects such as 4 pigs and 2 counters equals 6 'things'. Always make sure that the two groups of objects can be combined to make one set, for example 4 red cubes and 2 blue cubes is 6 cubes altogether.

Activities

❶ **Add two groups.**
Children work in pairs with one dice. The first child rolls, for example, a 5 and collects five things from the pile. The second child rolls, for example, a 2 and collects two things. They count each set and then combine them, counting the total. They create an adding sentence: 5 buttons add 2 buttons equals 7 buttons, or 5 add 2 equals 7.

30

❷ **Add three groups.**
Put a large hoop in the middle of the table.
Place two items (for example, two shells)
close together in one part of the hoop. *How
many shells are there in the hoop?* Ask a child
to count them. Place another three shells
close together in a different part of the hoop.
*How many more shells have I just put in the
hoop?* Place another four shells in a different
part of the hoop. *How many more shells have
I just put in the hoop? How many shells are in
the hoop altogether?* Push the shells together

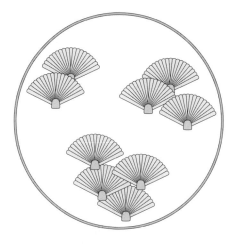

and ask a child to count them. Describe this as: *Two shells and three more makes
five shells and four more makes nine shells. Two and three and four makes nine.
Two add three add four is nine.* Demonstrate this by separating the objects into their
original groups and putting them back together as you describe the process. Repeat
for other start numbers (3, 4 or 5) and add two further sets to each. Emphasize the
numbers in each case: *Four shells and three shells and five shells is how many
shells?* (12) *So four add three add five is how many altogether?*

Feedback

Does each child appreciate that adding is when groups are combined?

Can each child answer simple addition questions involving two and three numbers?

Can anyone say the addition sentence without being prompted?

Do children use words such as 'plus', 'add' or 'total'?

Adding and subtracting

Objective

Relate addition to counting on.

Resources

▸ gameboard from **PCM 6**
▸ counters
▸ dice or 1–4 number cards
▸ feely bag
▸ cubes

What children are learning

to add numbers by counting on from a start number

Words you can use

and, makes, add, plus, equals, altogether, total, count, count on

Things to note

▸ There are many different ways of answering addition questions. An early approach involves combining two groups and finding the total. Another way is to count on a certain number of steps from a start number.

▸ When counting on, children often make errors because they start counting from the number they are on, rather than from the next number, for example given the addition 3 + 2, children might count on two by saying 'three, four' rather than 'four, five'. Encourage children to think of the *jumps* as being the things they are counting.

▸ Children do not need to read or write addition statements such as 3 + 4 = 7 at this stage. It is important that they have plenty of experience of counting on from one number to a larger number.

Activities

❶ Counting on.

Ask children to count in unison to fifteen, starting from one. Point to a child and say *One*. Ask the next child to say *Two* and so on. Continue the count around the group to fifteen. Repeat several times, starting with a different child each time. Ask a child to start counting aloud, then ask different children to take over the counting.

❷ Relate addition to counting on.

▸ Show the empty feely bag to the children. Put two cubes into the bag, one at a time, asking the children to count along. *How many cubes are in the bag?* If anyone is unsure, tip out the two cubes and start again. Add three more cubes to the bag, one at a time. *How many cubes are in the bag now?* Repeat several times, always starting with two cubes and then adding two, three, four etc. When children are confident, change the start number to three or four and continue to add different numbers of cubes.

▸ Use the gameboard on **PCM 6**. Place a counter for each child on the start. Children take turns to roll the dice and move forwards along the number track. Ask children to describe each move they make in the following way: 'I am on three, I move on two and land on five.' Describe each child's move using addition vocabulary: *Three add two makes five* or *Three plus two equals five*.

Variation: children could use a shorter number track, for example 1–20 if more appropriate and 1–4 number cards instead of a dice.

Feedback

Can each child add numbers by counting on from a start number?

When using the gameboard, did anyone predict the number they would land on before counting?

When counting to fifteen, was anyone hesitant or unsure?

Counting and reading numbers

Objective

Recite the number names in order, counting on or back from ten or nine.

Resources

‣ drum
‣ 1–20 number cards

What children are learning

to continue a number count

Words you can use

number, counting, zero, one, two ... twenty, before, after, next, count on

Things to note

▸ Children of a young age learn to recognize and recite the numbers in order, beginning first at one, then at zero. To begin reciting the numbers starting at any small number is an extra step for them. This can affect the rhythm and pattern of words that children have learnt and so can prove difficult for some.

▸ Children may find moving to a beat and counting at the same time more difficult than when counting while sitting down. At first their attention may be on marching and listening to the beat rather than on counting. With practice, however, children become confident with this activity.

▸ Controlling and varying the speed at which a child says the number names is also important in helping them to move beyond just saying the numbers as a rhyme. Children have to adjust the speed at which they say number names when they begin to count objects and sounds.

Activities

❶ **Recite number names in order forwards and backwards.**

▸ Ask some 'what comes next?' questions such as *Three, four, five, what comes next? Four, five, six, what comes next? Five, six, seven, what comes next?* If children are confident with saying their number names in order, questions can include counting forwards from other numbers to ten: *Seven, eight, nine, what comes next?* or counting backwards: *Eight, seven, six, what comes next?*

'… five, six, seven …'

- Share out a set of 1–20 number cards. Ask each child in turn to lay a card on the table and say the number aloud. Help children to place the cards in order (some may find this difficult) so that a 1–20 number track is spread across the table. Keeping the cards in the same positions, turn them face down, starting at one and counting along as you do so. Once the cards are face down, ask a child to turn over three consecutive cards. Invite children to say the three cards. *Can you count on from here? Can you count backwards from here?* Reveal the cards to check. Repeat for other sequences, giving each child a turn at choosing the three start numbers.
- Take the children to an area where they can move around freely. Use a drum to tap a beat for the children to march to. As you hit the drum, call out a number and a direction, for example *Ten, backwards!* Children must keep marching but continue to count backwards from ten until you call *Stop!* Repeat for other numbers. Vary the speed of the beat to make this activity more difficult.

Feedback

Can each child recite the number names in order, continuing from nine or ten forwards and backwards?

Did anyone find any numbers (such as 13–19) difficult to name when cards were turned over?

Was anyone who could count forwards confidently, unsure when counting backwards?

33 Counting and reading numbers

Objective

Recognize figures 1 to 9.

Resources

- 1–9 number cards
- 3 × 3 bingo grids of the figures 1–9 (see below for example)
- 1–9 number name cards
- gameboard from **PCM 5**, enlarged to A3 if possible
- dice

What children are learning

to match the figures from 1 to 9 with their number names

Words you can use

number, one, two … ten, count

Things to note

- Children sometimes find it difficult to relate their understanding of numbers to abstract squiggles on a page. Feeling the shapes of the figures made from felt, sandpaper or other textures is useful (see spread 27).
- Discuss the different figures in terms of whether they are made from straight or curved lines or a combination of the two, for example the figures 1, 4 and 7 are made only from straight lines, whilst 3, 6, 8 and 9 are made only from curved lines. Children sometimes confuse 2 and 5 because both are made from a mixture of curved and straight lines.

Activities

❶ **Recognize figures to 9.**

Provide each child with a 3 × 3 grid of figures 1–9, as shown. Each child's grid should show the figures in a different arrangement. Call out numbers from 1 to 9; children find this number in their grid and place a counter on it. The winner is the first to get three in a line covered with counters.

5	7	4
2	I	8
6	3	q

▶ *Variation: provide figures of a different range, for example repeated figures of 1–5, or figures from 10 to 20, according to the children's needs.*

33

❷ Match the number names to the figures.

Spread out the 1–9 number cards and corresponding number name cards face down on the table. Children take turns to turn over one card from each set, trying to find a matching pair. If the number name and figure match, the cards are put to one side; otherwise they are turned face down again and the next child has a turn. Assist children with reading the number names where necessary.

❸ Recognize figures to 9 and then count that many sounds or movements.

Use the gameboard on **PCM 5**, enlarged to A3 if possible. Place a counter for each child on the 'Start here' box on the gameboard. Children take turns to roll the dice and move forwards the right number of boxes. On landing on an instruction square, for example *Clap* or *Blink* etc., the child takes a 1–9 number card, says the number aloud and performs the action that many times, for example claps seven times. The card should then be replaced at the bottom of the pile.

Feedback

Can each child recognize and name the figures 1–9?

Did anyone have difficulty keeping count of actions?

Could anyone read the number names confidently?

34 Counting and reading numbers

Objectives
Count reliably to twenty.
Recognize figures 0 to 9.

Resources
- gameboard from **PCM 1**
- 0–9 number cards
- counters

What children are learning
- to say the number name that matches each figure between 0 and 9
- to count up to twenty objects reliably

Words you can use
count, one, two … twenty, number, number name

Things to note
- Some children find it difficult to point to objects one at a time as the number names are said. Count slowly and guide their finger if necessary. This action is known as *matching* or *one-to-one correspondence*, where one name is matched to one object. Eventually children should be able to match the name to an object without touching it.
- Children often confuse the figures 3 and 5, particularly when writing them themselves. Encourage children to trace the figures with their fingers or to write them in the air.

Activities
❶ **Recognize figures to 9.**
Shuffle several sets of 0–9 number cards together. Children take turns to pick a card. If the child can name the figure correctly they keep the card. The winner is the child with the most cards at the end.

34

❷ Recognize figures to 9 and count up to twenty objects.

Show the children the gameboard on **PCM 1** and explain that they are going to take turns to play. The game involves collecting counters from a pile and putting them

onto the stepping stones to reach the castle. Each child must count to ten to start their go. The child then takes a card from the pack and takes that many counters from a pile. Emphasize careful counting. The counters should be placed on the stepping stones, starting at one side of the river and gradually working towards the castle. The next player then counts to ten, picks a card and adds their counters to those on the trail, working their way from the jetty across to the castle. After each go, encourage the children to count the number of counters on the trail until the number size

becomes too large for them. The winner is the player to put a counter on the last stepping stone to reach the castle.

Variation: 10–12 number cards could also be used if children are confident with the figures to 9.

❸ Count up to twenty objects.

Ask children in turn to count out different-sized sets of counters. Emphasize careful counting and then ask children to swap places with a friend and check how many counters they have.

Feedback

Can each child:

▸ say the number name for each figure from 0 to 9?
▸ count up to twenty objects reliably?

Who could count confidently past twenty?

Did anyone lack confidence in counting?

Adding and subtracting

Objective

Relate addition to counting on.

Resources

▸ dominoes

What children are learning

to add numbers by counting on from a start number

Words you can use

and, makes, add, plus, equals, altogether, total, count, count on

Things to note

▸ There are many different ways of answering addition questions. An early approach involves combining two groups and finding the total. Another way is that of counting on a certain number of steps from a start number.

▸ When counting on, children often make errors because they start counting from the number they are on, rather than from the next number, for example given the addition 3 + 2, children might count on two by saying 'three, four' rather than 'four, five'. Encourage children to think of the *jumps* as being the things they are counting.

▸ Children do not need to read or write addition statements such as 3 + 4 = 7 at this stage. It is important that they have plenty of experience of counting on from one number to a larger number.

Activities

❶ **Relate addition to counting on.**

▸ Hold up five fingers of one hand. Count them together. Hold up one finger on the other hand. *Five fingers on one hand and one on the other. How many fingers am I holding up?* Explain that we do not need to count all our fingers again. *We know we have five fingers on this hand, so five add one more is?* (6) Show children this with your fingers and invite them all to say with you: *Five add one is six.*

Ask children to hold up five fingers on one hand. *How many fingers on this hand?* Ask children to hold up two on the other hand. *How many fingers are you holding up altogether?* Encourage children to say *Five* and then to count on two steps: *Six, seven!* Point to a 0–10 number line and show that if we count on two jumps from five we reach seven.

▸ Repeat the activity above, asking children to hold up four fingers on one hand and two, three, or four on the other. *Remember we have four on this hand so we don't need to count them again. We just count on from this number.* Use the number line again to help children to check their answers.

▸ Spread out a set of dominoes on the table. Ask children to pick a domino and count the number of spots on each side. Ask them to tell the others about their domino, for example 'My domino has three spots on one side and four on the other side.'

Show children how to find the total number of spots by counting on from one number, for example counting on four jumps from three: *Four, five, six, seven!* Describe each child's move using addition vocabulary: *Three add four makes seven* or *Three plus four equals seven*.

Feedback

Can each child add numbers by counting on from a start number?

Note any children who could recognize spot patterns on dominoes and who did not need to count.

Which children used vocabulary such as 'add', 'plus' and 'equals' confidently?

Money and 'real life' problems

Objectives

Understand and use the vocabulary related to money.
Sort coins: 1p, 2p, 5p, 10p, 20p.
Use 1p coins in role play.

Resources

▸ 1p, 2p, 5p, 10p and 20p coins
▸ feely bag
▸ coin stamps
▸ five small containers labelled '1p', '2p', '5p', '10p' and '20p'
▸ shop items labelled with prices '1p', '2p' and '3p'

What children are learning

▸ to recognize and name 1p, 2p, 5p, 10p and 20p coins
▸ to sort the coins into groups
▸ to use 1p coins to make different totals

Words you can use

sort, set, coins, 1p, 2p, 5p, 10p, 20p, pence, penny, how many?, total, cost, pay, price, count, number, more, fewer

Things to note

▸ Some children may already be familiar with money, but may require plenty of practice in making different totals with 1p coins.
▸ Real coins are preferred for this type of activity, although plastic coins are acceptable. If plastic coins are used, show real coins to the children to help them see how these differ from the plastic ones.

Activities

❶ **Recognize 1p, 2p, 5p, 10p and 20p coins.**

▸ Put several 1p, 2p, 5p, 10p and 20p coins into a feely bag. Children take turns to take a coin from the bag. The winner is the first child to collect one of each of the coins. Children can then arrange the coins in order of value, to emphasize that their value is not related to their actual size.

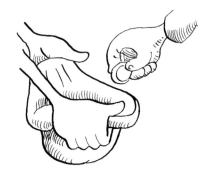

▸ Use coin stamps to make pictures of the coins in the children's books or on paper and ask them to colour the coins and to write the name of the coin: 1p, 2p etc. Some children may need assistance with writing these. Alternatively, children could make rubbings of the coins.

❷ **Sort 1p, 2p, 5p, 10p and 20p coins.**
Place a mixture of 1p, 2p, 5p, 10p and 20p coins in a pile in the middle of the table. Ask a child to find a 1p coin. Ask questions about it: *What shape is it? Is it silver? How much is it worth?* Repeat for the other coins. Using five labelled yogurt pots or similar containers, tell the children that a shopkeeper wants to sort the money into separate groups of coins. Ask them to take turns to pick up a coin, say which coin it is and place it into the correct pot.

❸ **Use 1p coins.**
You will need some 'shop' items such as plastic cakes, biscuits, sweets etc. labelled '1p', '2p' or '3p'. Give each child several 1p coins and make one child the shopkeeper. Children buy an item from the shopkeeper by giving the exact number of pennies to pay for the item. The shopkeeper must check carefully. Allow children time to shop and pay, asking them questions such as *Have you enough money to buy the cake? How many pennies do you need? How much money have you now?*

Feedback

Can each child:
▸ recognize 1p, 2p, 5p, 10p and 20p coins?
▸ sort 1p, 2p, 5p, 10p and 20p coins?
▸ use 1p coins to pay for items costing 1p, 2p or 3p?

Did anyone talk about the values of coins saying, for example, 'a 10p coin is worth the same as ten ones'?

Did anyone have difficulty putting the coins in order of value?

Counting, reading and writing numbers

Objective

Say and use number names beyond twenty in order in contexts, for example number rhymes, songs, counting games and activities.

Resources

▸ one copy of **PCM 6**

What children are learning

to learn the pattern of the number names to twenty and beyond

Words you can use

count, number, one, two ... thirty, number name

Things to note

▸ The number names beyond ten do not follow a simple pattern. Children need to begin to recognize that not all the 'teen' numbers are made in the same way. Fourteen, sixteen, seventeen, eighteen and nineteen are the single numbers four, six, seven, eight and nine followed with 'teen'. Unfortunately thirteen and fifteen are not 'threeteen' and 'fiveteen'! Make sure that children say 'teen' clearly, and not thirty, forty etc.

▸ As children become more familiar with the numbers ask them to listen for counting errors, spoken perhaps by a puppet, for example *Fourteen, 'fifteen', sixteen, seventeen, eighteen, nineteen, 'tenteen'... Twenty-seven, twenty-eight, twenty-nine, 'twenty-ten'.*

▸ The number names beyond twenty do follow a simple pattern, twenty followed by one, two, three etc. up to twenty-nine. This pattern is generally learned by hearing the rhythm of the words.

37

Activities

❶ Say and use number names in order up to twenty and beyond.

▸ Say the following number rhyme asking children to join in with appropriate actions.

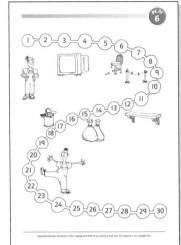

There's so much to do!

I make and mend things round the house
I've lots to do today
I've got so many jobs I must get done
There's just no time for play!

1, 2, 3	*I must mend the TV*
4, 5, 6	*This chair leg I must fix*
7, 8, 9	*I'll mend the washing line*
10, 11, 12	*I'll put up Sally's shelf*
13, 14, 15	*This rubbish here needs shifting*
16, 17, 18	*I'll do a bit of painting*
19, 20, 21	*I've done my jobs, my day is done!*

▸ Show **PCM 6** to the children and say the rhyme again. Ask a child to point to the numbers on the trail as the rhyme is spoken. This encourages them to make the link between number names and figures. Then ask individuals to say the numbers in the rhyme when you point to the figures.

▸ Using the number trail, explore the numbers beyond twenty, asking children to say the numbers in unison from twenty-one up to thirty. Keep a steady rhythm to help children learn the pattern of words.

Feedback

Can each child:

▸ say the number names in order up to twenty?
▸ say the number names in order beyond twenty?

Did anyone wait to be prompted by others when saying the numbers?

Did anyone volunteer to count past thirty?

38 Comparing and ordering numbers

Objective

Order a given set of selected numbers (for example 2, 5, 8, 1, 4).

Resources

‣ 0–9 number cards for each child
‣ washing line and pegs

What children are learning

to order a set of numbers from 0 to 9

Words you can use

order, count, number, zero, one, two … nine, more, less, greater, smaller

Things to note

‣ In order to arrange a set of numbers in order, children must first appreciate which of two numbers is greater and which is smaller.
‣ Children also need to begin to recognize figures. If children cannot match the number name with the figure, tell them what the figure is called. Number name cards could be placed in order if more appropriate for the children.
‣ Children could be provided with a number line or track to assist them in these activities.

Activities

❶ **Order numbers to at least twenty.**
  ‣ Shuffle a set of 0–9 number cards and place them face down in a pile in the middle of the table; stretch the 'washing line' across a table or hang it where the children can reach. Explain to the children that they are going to put some of the numbers from 0 to 9 on this line, with the larger numbers nearer the right-hand end and smaller numbers at the left-hand end. Each child turns over a card and tries to put the number in the correct place on the washing line. It may be necessary to move numbers already on the line. *What number is that? Is it greater or less than five? Which end of the line do you think it will be closer to?*

84

38

After each child's turn ask the children to say the numbers in order from 0 to 9 to check that the numbers on the line appear in the correct order. Ask children to work out which numbers are missing. *Which numbers are not on the line? Where would six go?*

▸ Shuffle several sets of 0–9 number cards together. Give five cards to each child and put the remainder in a pile face down in the middle of the table. Children look at their own cards and say 'snap' if any two are the same. They must then swap one of these cards for a replacement from the pile until each child has five *different* numbers. The children should place their cards side by side in order. They can then copy the numbers in order into their exercise books.

▶ *Variations: children can be given fewer cards (three or four) if they are less confident with ordering numbers. Where necessary, 0–12 or 0–20 number cards could be used to provide more of a challenge.*

Feedback

Can each child order a set of three, four or five numbers from the range 0–9?

Did anyone confuse two numbers such as 2 and 5?

In the washing-line game, was anyone trying to correct other players, for example saying where gaps should be left?

Counting, reading and writing numbers

Objective

Recognize figures 0 to 10.

Resources

- figures 0 and 1 made from felt, sandpaper or plastic
- number line or track
- cubes
- pasta shells or similar
- 0–10 number cards
- 3 × 3 bingo grids of the figures 1–10 (see below for example)
- 0–10 number name cards

What children are learning

to match the figures 0–10 with their number names

Words you can use

number, zero, one, two … ten, count, number name

Things to note

- Children sometimes find it difficult to relate their understanding of numbers to abstract squiggles on a page. Encourage children to trace the figures with their fingers or to write them in the air. The use of felt or sandpaper figures is recommended because children develop a 'feel' for the number.
- Discuss whether the different figures are made from straight or curved lines or a combination of the two. For example, the figures 1, 4 and 7 are made only from straight lines, whilst 3, 6, 8 and 9 are made only from curved lines. Children sometimes confuse 2 and 5 because they are made from both curved and straight lines.

Activities

❶ **Introduce the figures 0 and 10.**
Place the 0 and 1 figures made from felt, sandpaper or plastic on the table. Pass round the zero. *What number is this?* Ask children to make the circular shape with their finger in the air. Show the one. *What number is this?* Point to a number line or track to show that zero and one are next to each other when we count. Tell the children that when the one and the zero are written next to each other, this stands for a completely different number. *What number is written as 'one zero'?* Place the digits side by side and ask the children to say 'ten' in unison.

❷ Recognize figures from 0 to 10.

▸ Write the figures 0–10 randomly on a piece of paper as in the example here and cover each figure with a cube. Ask a child to lift a cube and say the number name. The child should then collect that number of pasta shells from a central pile. The next child lifts a cube, says the number name and collects that number of pasta shells. Continue until all the figures are uncovered. *Who do you think has the most shells?*

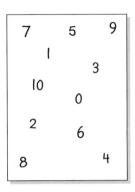

▸ Provide each child with a different 3 × 3 grid of some of the figures from 0 to 10, arranged in any order. An example is shown here. Call out numbers from zero to ten; children look for the number in their grid and place a counter on it. The winner is the child to get three in a line covered with counters.

10	7	4
2	1	0
6	3	9

❸ Match the number names to the figures.

Spread out the 1–10 number cards and corresponding number name cards face down on the table. Children take turns to turn over one card from each set, trying to find a matching pair. If the number name and figure match, the cards are put to one side; otherwise they are turned face down again and the next child has a turn. Assist children with reading the number names where necessary.

Feedback

Can each child recognize and name the figures from 0 to 10?

Who could read the number names confidently?

Was anyone hesitant or unsure in any of the activities?

Objectives

Begin to relate addition of doubles to counting on.
Find a total by counting on when one group is hidden.

Resources

▸ a magic wand!
▸ cubes
▸ piece of cloth or a handkerchief
▸ copy of **PCM 4** for each child
▸ dominoes

What children are learning

▸ to understand what doubling is
▸ to add doubles by counting on from one number, rather than counting both numbers
▸ to begin to understand that a double can be found even if you can't see one group

Words you can use

double, number, count, how many, one … twenty, adding, plus, makes, altogether, total

Things to note

▸ Children need to begin to appreciate that it is not necessary to see both halves of a number to be doubled because both halves are the same. When they are doubling a number they can start on the number and count on the same number of steps.

Activities

❶ **Introduce doubling.**

▸ Introduce the children to the idea of a magician with a magic wand. Place a stick of two yellow cubes on the table for the children to see. Then cover this with a piece of cloth and wave the magic wand. Secretly place a second stick of two cubes underneath. Reveal *two* sticks of yellow cubes! *This trick is known as doubling. There were two cubes and now there are double the number of cubes*. Ask children to count how many cubes there are now. Encourage them to use a counting-on method, where they do not need to count one of the sets of two, rather they start counting on from two: *Three, four. Double two is four*.

▸ Perform the trick again, this time doubling a set of three cubes. *There were three cubes and now there are double the number of cubes*. Ask children to count how many cubes there are now, again using a counting-on method: *Four, five, six. Double three is six*. Record the doubles on the board or on a large piece of paper: double 2 is 4, double 3 is 6. Repeat for double 1 and double 4.

❷ **Draw doubles and find the total.**
Show children some 'double' dominoes, for example 6,6; 3,3. *How many spots are on this domino altogether?* Encourage children to count on from six or three. Give children a copy of **PCM 4** and ask them to draw spots onto the dominoes so that each domino is a 'double' domino. They can copy dominoes from the real set. As they draw each domino ask them to find and tell you the total; they can write the total underneath using figures if they are familiar with them.

❸ **Hide one part of the double and find the total.**
Once children have become familiar with doubles and counting on to find the total, show them a double domino and cover one half. *This domino shows double three. How could we find the total number of spots without me lifting my hand from this side?* Encourage children to see that you can put the number in your head and then count on that many: *Keep three in your head and count on three more: four, five, six!* Choose a few more double dominoes to test this approach.

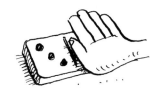

Feedback

Does each child understand what doubling is?

Can each child:
▸ add doubles by counting on from one number?
▸ appreciate that a double can be found even if you can't see one group?

Ask individual children questions such as *Can you explain what a double is? Can you find a double on a domino? How did you know which one to take?* Note what each child says.

Objective

Write figures to 5.

Resources

▸ 0–5 number cards
▸ cubes or counters
▸ pencil and paper

What children are learning

to correctly write figures 0–5, forming the figures in the correct way (see below)

Words you can use

digit, number, zero, one, two … five

Things to note

▸ Writing figures can be quite difficult for children. Common errors include reversing the numbers, and confusing figures such as 3 and 5.
▸ Encourage children to trace the figures with their fingers or to write them in the air. When writing the figures 3 and 5, begin at the top left-hand corner and work to the right and down, returning to put the top stroke on the 5 at the end. Ensure that children always begin to write the figure from the correct position and move in the correct direction. (See diagrams for reference.)
▸ The use of felt or sandpaper figures is recommended because children develop a 'feel' for the number.

Activities

❶ Read figures from 0 to 5.

> ▸ Place a pile of cubes or counters on the table. Ask children to pick a 0–5 number card and to read it aloud to the group. *Who has the largest number? Who has the smallest?* Ask them to hold them up in turn from zero to five. *Who's got number three? Who's got the number that comes after three? What is it called? What number comes before three?*

> ▸ Ask children to take their number of objects from the pile, and to put them on the table next to their card. Check around the group, asking children to count each collection.

❷ Write figures from 0 to 5.

Ask children to draw their number of objects on paper and to write the figure alongside. Repeat as necessary, allowing children to draw and write all the figures from 0 to 5. If a child reverses their figure, help them to trace the figure correctly and guide the child's hand to draw the figure several times. It may be necessary to restrict some children to the figures 1 to 3 or 4 initially. Watch the way that children are forming the figures, checking the starting point and direction to ensure that children develop good habits.

Feedback

Can each child write figures to 5, forming them correctly?

Ask each child to look at their own work and to decide which numbers are written most carefully. Can they write any of the numbers even more carefully? Note which children are able to assess and improve upon their own work.

42 Counting, reading and writing numbers

Objective
Count and record larger numbers by tallying.

Resources
- twelve objects, for example toy car, box, sandal etc.
- a bag for the objects or access to a sandpit
- paper
- cubes

What children are learning
- to make their own marks or tallies to record numbers in practical situations
- to count their marks or tallies accurately

Words you can use
record, count, number, one, two … twenty, how many?, mark, tally

Things to note
- When trying to count a range of items, children need to appreciate that it is sometimes easier to make marks on a piece of paper and count those. It is important that the correct number of marks is made.
- At this stage the marks could be quick drawings of the objects, or just lines or crosses. Children are not expected to use a more formal tallying approach in which the fifth line crosses the previous four. This is a skill that children will develop later.

Activities
❶ **Count and record larger numbers by tallying.**
- Place at least twelve objects in a bag (or bury them in a sandpit). Explain to the children that they are going to find all the objects and record the number of things they find. Give each child a sheet of paper and ask them to make a mark on the paper as each object is found. Tell them that drawing a line is a 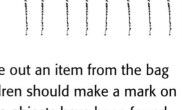 quick way of recording. Ask each child in turn to take out an item from the bag (or sandpit) and to show it to everyone. All the children should make a mark on their piece of paper. Continue in this way until all the objects have been found and recorded.

42

- *How many marks have you got on your piece of paper?* Ask each child to count their marks carefully. *Do we all have the same answer? Who do you think has got the right answer?* Do not tell children how many objects there are at this point. Take each item and place it back in the bag (or sandpit) and ask the children to count with you as you do so. *How many items are there? Do you have the right number of marks on your piece of paper?*
- Give each child a large handful of cubes and ask them to make marks to count in the same way. Explain that this time they may all have different numbers of cubes, so their answers will be different. Encourage children to make simple marks rather than more complex drawings.

Feedback

Can each child:

- make their own marks or tallies to record numbers?
- count their marks or tallies accurately?

Did anyone need help to remember to record when others took an object from the bag?

Was anyone systematic, for example keeping their marks in lines to make them easy to count?

43 Counting, reading and writing numbers

Objective

Count in tens.

Resources

▸ 10–100 number track
▸ copy of **PCM 7**, enlarged to A3 if possible
▸ 1–100 square

What children are learning

the patterns of the multiples of ten: ten, twenty, thirty …

Words you can use

count on, add, plus, altogether, more, makes, equals, ten, twenty … one hundred, tens, units or ones

Things to note

▸ Children need experience of counting on and back in tens to become familiar with the 'multiples' of ten: ten, twenty, thirty … and to begin to realize that they are ten apart. These multiples of ten are also significant because, beyond twenty, all the numbers up to 100 follow the pattern '…ty-one', '…ty-two', '…ty-three' and so on.
▸ Emphasize the connection between counting on in tens and 'adding ten' and use a range of vocabulary to describe this: *forty plus ten, forty and ten more, forty add ten, forty and ten altogether makes …*
▸ Children may fall into a pattern when saying the numbers so that they say 'ten-ty', following 'eight-ty' and 'nine-ty'.

Activities

❶ **Count on in tens.**

▸ Show children **PCM 7**, enlarged to A3 if possible. *What are these numbers? Can anyone tell me the names of any of these numbers?* Children may be unfamiliar with the figures, so count along the track. *We call this counting in tens. Each jump is a jump of ten.* Ask children to join in with you and count on in tens several times. *What do you notice about each of these numbers?* Point out that each number ends in a zero.

▸ Show the children a 1–100 square. *Can you find these numbers anywhere on this hundred square?* Help children to find the numbers and count again in tens from 10 to 100.

43

❷ Count on in tens from any multiple of ten.
Play the following game using **PCM 7** and two cards marked '10' and '0'. Place a counter for each child at the start. Children turn over one of the cards and move forward that many places (that is, either one or no places). Children may start to count on ten places, so remind them that each step is worth ten. Encourage and help them to describe their move: *What number have you landed on? Ten and ten more is twenty* etc. The winner is the first child to reach 100.

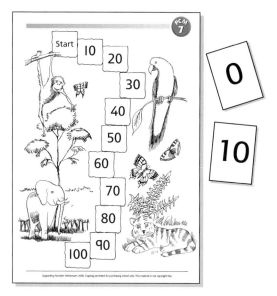

❸ Keep a record of the number of tens counted.
Use **PCM 7** to help children count on a certain number of tens, for example *Count on in tens from ten and stop at thirty. How many tens did you count?* (2) *Count on in tens from forty. Stop. How many tens did you count?* Ask questions for children to work out, for example *Start on ten, add ten, add ten, add ten. Where do you end up?* (40) Invite a child to show these jumps using a counter on the board.

▷ *Variation: the activities above can be repeated for counting back in tens.*

Feedback

Can each child:
▸ count on in tens up to 100?
▸ count on a certain number of tens, for example four tens starting at ten?

Who could describe their move without prompting? For example, *I was on twenty; twenty and ten more is thirty*.

Counting, reading and writing numbers

Objective
Recognize figures beyond 10.

Resources
- 4 × 4 bingo grids of the figures 0–20 (see below for example)
- counters
- **PCM 6**
- dice

What children are learning
to recognize figures to 15, 20 or 30

Words you can use
number, zero, one, two … ten etc., count, number name

Things to note
- Children sometimes find it difficult to relate their understanding of numbers to abstract squiggles on a page. Encourage children to trace the figures with their fingers or to write them in the air. The use of felt or sandpaper figures is recommended because children develop a 'feel' for the number.
- Discuss whether the different figures are made from straight or curved lines or a combination of the two, for example the figures 1, 4 and 7 are made only from straight lines, whilst 3, 6, 8 and 9 are made only from curved lines. Children sometimes confuse 2 and 5 because they are made from both curved and straight lines.

Activities
❶ **Recognize figures from 0 to 10.**
- Put a pile of cubes in the middle of the table. Ask children to pick a 0–10 number card in turn and read it aloud to the group. *Who has the largest number? Who has the smallest?* Ask children to hold their cards up in turn from zero to ten. *Who's got number five? Who's got the number that comes after five? What is it called? What number comes before five?*
- Ask children to gather their number of cubes from the pile, and to join the cubes to make a stick. The stick should be placed on the table next to their card. Check around the group, asking children to compare sticks.

❷ **Read figures beyond 10.**

▸ Provide each child with a 4 × 4 grid of some of the figures from 0 to 20, arranged in any order, as shown. Each child's grid should show a different arrangement of figures. Call out number names from zero to twenty and ask children to look for the number in their grid and place a counter on it. The winner is the child to get three in a line covered with counters. Ask children to point to the figures in order and to say which are missing.

5	12	4	11
2	7	8	18
6	20	15	9
13	3	19	14

▷ *Variation: provide a smaller grid with fewer figures, for example 1–12 or 1–10 as appropriate.*

▸ Use the gameboard on **PCM 6**. Give each child a different coloured counter. Children take turns to throw the dice and count on that number of spaces along the track. They then say aloud the number they have landed on.

Feedback

Can each child:

▸ recognize figures to 15?

▸ recognize figures to 20?

▸ recognize figures to 30?

Was anyone hesitant or unsure in any activity?

When comparing sticks of cubes, did anyone volunteer phrases such as 'one more than', 'two less than'?

45 Adding and subtracting

Objective

Remove a smaller number from a larger number and find how many are left by counting back from the larger number.

Resources

- counters
- hoop
- 6–10 number cards
- dice

What children are learning

to remove a smaller number from a larger number and find how many are left by counting back from the larger number, for example 8 take away 3; count back seven, six, five

Words you can use

subtract, minus, take away, number, number track

Things to note

- Subtraction questions can be solved in many ways. These include removing objects and counting those left; counting on from the smaller to the larger number; and this strategy which involves counting back from the larger number to the smaller number.
- For this strategy it is important that children concentrate on counting back from the start number to find how many are left. The remaining counters should be covered so children do count back. If they can see the remaining counters they will simply count those rather than counting back.

Activities

❶ **Remove a smaller number from a larger number and find how many are left by counting back from the larger number.**

- Put five counters in a hoop. Take two counters out of the hoop and place them nearby. Cover the three counters remaining in the hoop. *How many counters are in the hoop?* If children are unsure, point to 5 on the 0–10 number track. *How many did I take away? Two. So let's count back two.* Jump back to 4 and then to 3, saying *four, three. Five take away two is three. There are three counters in the hoop.* Uncover the counters to check. Repeat several times, for example 6 – 3; 4 – 2; 7 – 4.

▸ Use 6–10 number cards and a dice. Ask a child to turn over a card to provide the start number and to put this in the middle of the table. Children take turns to roll the dice and to count back this many from the start number. Describe the situation each time using subtraction vocabulary, for example *Eight subtract three; eight take away three; eight minus three*. When all children have rolled the dice change the start number. Allow children to use the number track to check their counting back.

▸ *Variations: instead of rolling a dice, children can find the number to be subtracted by picking a 0–6 number card. Start numbers can be extended to include numbers beyond ten and children can subtract using 0–10 number cards.*

Feedback

Can each child remove a smaller number from a larger number and find how many are left by counting back from the larger number?

Which children used subtraction vocabulary to say what they did?

Make sure each child has a chance to use the number track themselves, rather than just watching you. Did anyone have difficulty knowing where to start or stop?

Money and 'real life' problems

Objectives

Sort all coins, including £1 and £2, and use in role play.
Solve practical problems.

Resources

- 1p, 2p, 5p, 10p, 20p, 50p, £1 and £2 coins
- feely bag
- eight small containers, each labelled for one type of coin
- selection of small and large shop items

What children are learning

- to recognize and name the coins 1p, 2p, 5p, 10p, 20p, 50p, £1 and £2
- to sort the coins into groups
- to use 1p coins to make different totals

Words you can use

sort, set, coins, 1p, 2p, 5p, 10p, 20p, 50p, £1 and £2, pound, pence, penny, how many?, total, cost, pay, price, count, number, more, fewer

Things to note

- Some children may already be familiar with money, but may require plenty of practice in making different totals with the coins.
- Real coins are preferred for this type of activity, although plastic coins are acceptable. If plastic coins are used, show real coins to the children to help them see how these differ from the plastic ones and to gain a feel for the weight of the coins.

Activities

❶ **Recognize all the coins.**
Put several of each coin into a feely bag. Children take turns to take a coin from the bag. The winner is the first child to collect four different coins. Children can arrange their coins in order of value, to emphasize that their value is not related to their actual size.

❷ Sorting coins.

Place a mixture of coins in a pile in the middle of the table and have ready eight labelled containers (or labelled sheets of paper). Tell the children that a shopkeeper wants to sort the money into separate groups of coins. Children take turns to choose a coin, say which coin it is and put it in the correct pot.

❸ Solve practical problems using role play.

▸ You will need some 'shop' items, for example plastic cakes, biscuits, sweets etc. and some larger items, for example a jumper, a pair of shoes etc. The items do not need to be labelled. Designate one child as the shopkeeper. Give each child five coins and ask them to buy five items. The buyer shows their chosen item to the shopkeeper, together with their five coins. The shopkeeper names one of these coins as the price of the item and the buyer hands over the appropriate coin. Another child then takes a turn. Encourage the shopkeeper to price items appropriately, for example the larger items might be more expensive.

▸ Allow children time to shop and pay, asking them questions such as *How much do you think it will cost? How many coins have you? Which coins are they?*

Feedback

Can each child:

▸ recognize all coins?

▸ sort coins?

▸ use coins appropriately in role play?

In the role play, did anyone compare their five coins with another player's and work out who had more money?

Did anyone show that they understood the relative values of the coins?

Counting, reading and writing numbers

Objective
Estimate a number up to ten and check by counting.

Resources
▸ a selection of small items such as cubes, counters, buttons and beads
▸ a handkerchief, cloth or piece of paper

What children are learning
▸ to gain an idea of how many things there are without counting, which helps to develop a 'feel' for numbers
▸ that an estimate doesn't need to be exact but, instead, just needs to give a reasonable idea of the actual number

Words you can use
estimate, think, guess, nearly, about, close to, more than, less than, roughly

Things to note
▸ Emphasize that an estimate doesn't have to give the exact number; it is more of a 'good guess' to get a sense of how many there are. Avoid praising only the estimates that are 'spot on'; instead praise any estimate that is a 'good guess'. If children think they have to be 'spot on' they can be reluctant to estimate, preferring to count first and then pretend to have estimated the exact number.
▸ When estimating, people sometimes get clues from the arrangement of the objects, for example knowing that there are five in the arrangement shown on a dice. Looking for patterns of this type can help in making a good estimate.

47

Activities

❶ Estimate up to ten objects.

▸ *Who is good at guessing? We're going to play a guessing game today.* Take a small handful of objects, for example seven buttons, and place them on the table. After 3–4 seconds, cover them with a cloth or piece of paper. *How many buttons are under the cloth? Why do you think that number? Did anyone count them? Why? If there isn't time to count them what can you do?* Ask children to try to 'think' the number without counting. Collect the estimates from around the group and then uncover and count the items. Repeat several times, giving children long enough to get a sense of the number of objects but not long enough to count them. Extend the activity to include sets of different items to estimate, for example a mixture of buttons, conkers and matchsticks. *How many things are on the table?*

▸ Ask children to estimate numbers of objects around the room and record this, for example by drawing a pencil pot and then writing how many they think there are in the room. Some children may need assistance in writing the figure for the number they estimate.

Feedback

Can each child give a sensible estimate of up to ten objects?

Was anyone reluctant to give an estimate because they were anxious about giving the wrong answer?

Did anyone use the arrangement of the objects to help them make an estimate (for example, four chairs around a table)?

48 Comparing and ordering numbers

Objective

Begin to understand and use ordinal numbers in different contexts.

Resources

▸ number cards for the number of children in the group
▸ beads in a range of colours
▸ thread

What children are learning

▸ to relate the numbers 1, 2, 3, 4 etc to first, second, third, fourth etc.
▸ to put ordinal numbers to 5 or 10 in order, that is numbers that show order, as in first, second, third etc.

Words you can use

first, second, third, fourth etc., next to, between, last

Things to note

▸ Ordinal numbers are those that we use to describe the order of a set of items: first, second, third and so on. They are closely linked to the counting numbers one, two, three and so on. Children at this stage need to learn the words and relate them to the numbers.
▸ Note that ordinal numbers that end with a 'th' relate to numbers 4–10. The numbers relating to one, two and three do not follow the pattern of saying the number and adding a 'th' as in 'four-th'. Note also that fifth is not 'fiveth'. This can confuse children learning to say the ordinal numbers, particularly when counting backwards. Errors include: eighth, seventh, sixth, 'fiveth', fourth, 'threeth', 'twoth'.

Activities

❶ **Standing in line.**

▸ Ask the children to count in unison to twenty and then individually around the group. Give each child a number card, starting at 1 and continuing to the number of children in the group (5, for example). *We're going to stand in a line. Who has the number one? Come and stand next to me. You are first in the line. Number one is first. Who comes next? Number two. Stand behind number one. You are second in the line. Number two is second. Who is next? Number three. You are third in the line.* When the line is complete, point to each child in turn, saying *first, second, third* etc. *Who is third in the line? Who is fourth?*

48

> Take the number cards from the children and rearrange the line. *Let's pretend you are all waiting to see me. Who is first in the line? Who is second? How many are behind him/her?* Rearrange the line again and ask: *Who is third in the line to see me? How many are in front of him/her? John, what position are you in the line? What position is between third and fifth? Who is last? Who is next to last?*

❷ **Order and describe strings of beads.**

> Ask children to thread up to ten beads (if appropriate) in alternating colours onto a string, for example red, white, red, white … Go through the beads in order: *What colour is the first bead you threaded? What colour is the second? The third?* etc. Now ask questions at random: *What colour is the fifth bead? The eighth?*

> Ask children to thread beads on your instructions: *First thread a blue one, then a green, then a black* and so on until each child has an identical string of beads.

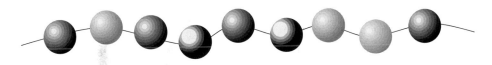

Ensuring that all children start from the same coloured bead, go through them in order: *What colour is the first bead you threaded? What colour is the second? The third?* and so on. When children are confident, ask *What position is the red bead? The yellow bead? The white bead?* etc. Allow each child to ask a question.

Feedback

Can each child use the ordinal numbers – first, second, third … tenth (or beyond)?

Who can talk about the line of children or the string of beads, making up sentences such as 'Jo is first in the line'; 'My third bead is red'?

Does anyone use first to third/fourth confidently, but then get stuck beyond that?

Objective

Count in twos.

Resources

▸ 0–10 number track
▸ toy frog and rabbit or similar

What children are learning

▸ to count in twos starting at zero
▸ to count in twos starting at one

Words you can use

count on, twos, zero, one, two … ten

Things to note

▸ Children may find counting in twos starting from one more difficult than starting from zero. Move onto this only when children are confident about counting in twos starting from zero.

Activities

❶ **Count in twos from zero.**

▸ Put a 0–10 number track on the table. Introduce a toy frog (or similar) and place it on the 0. Ask the children to count as the frog jumps in twos along the track to 10: *two, four, six, eight, ten.* Repeat the activity several times. Invite children to jump the frog along the line in the same way. *Let's make the frog jump in twos like this: two, four, six…*

▸ Sing rhymes with the children, for example:
Two, four, six, eight,
Meet me at the garden gate.
Two, four, six, eight,
If I'm late you can wait.
Two, four, six, eight, ten,
I am hiding in my den.
Two, four, six, eight, ten,
Now I'm coming out again.

49

▸ Ask children to count in unison from zero to ten. Explain that the first number should be said loudly, the second whispered, the third loudly and so on: ***zero, one, two,*** three, ***four,*** five … Repeat several times. Now count around the group individually in the same pattern.

❷ **Count in twos from one.**
▸ Use the number track again but with a different creature, for example a rabbit, doing the jumping. Start at one and jump on in twos to nine. Encourage children to count along with the rabbit: *One, three, five, seven, nine.* Repeat the activity several times. Invite children to jump the rabbit along the line in the same way. *Let's make the rabbit jump in twos like this: one, three, five …*
▸ Ask children to count in unison from one to nine, saying the first number loudly, the second quietly and so on: **one**, two, **three**, four, **five** … Repeat several times. Now count individually around the group in the same pattern.

Feedback

Can each child:
▸ count in twos from zero to ten or beyond?
▸ count in twos from one to nine or beyond?

Can anyone explain why you get different numbers if you start counting from one rather than zero?

Can anyone count in twos from zero and go past ten?

Can anyone close their eyes and count in twos from zero to ten or from one to nine?

Adding and subtracting

Objective

Begin to find how many have been removed from a group of objects by counting up from a number.

Resources

▸ 'number bears' made from **PCM 2**
▸ 0–10 number cards

What children are learning

to solve subtraction questions by counting up from the smaller number, for example
7 – 5: *six, seven*

Words you can use

subtract, minus, take away, number, count on

Things to note

▸ Subtraction questions can be solved in many ways. These include removing objects and counting those left; counting back from the larger number to the smaller number; and this strategy which involves counting on from the smaller number to the larger number.

▸ When counting on, children often make errors because they start counting from the number they are on, rather than from the next number. For example, when counting on from three to five, children might count up 'three, four, five' and give the answer three. Encourage the children to think of the *jumps* as being the things they are counting.

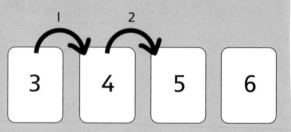

50

Activities

❶ Find how many have been removed from a group of objects by counting up from a number.

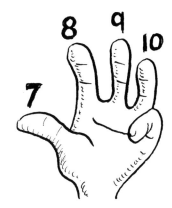

- ▸ Use 'number bears' made from **PCM 2**. Ask a child to count all the bears; remind children that there are ten bears in total. *If I hide six of the bears, how could I find out how many will be left?* Show children that one way is to count on from six up to ten: *Put the number six in your head and count on to ten on your fingers. How many fingers am I holding up? Ten bears take away six bears will leave us with four bears.* Show this using the number bears, asking children to count them. Repeat for 10 take away 7, 10 take away 5 and 10 take away 8, ensuring that children use the strategy of counting on from the smaller number, using their fingers to count how many more to make ten.

- ▸ Put 6–10 number cards in one pile and 1–5 number cards in another pile. Children take turns to turn over one card from each pile to create a subtraction question such as 9 take away 4. Encourage children to start at the smaller number and count up to the larger number, remembering to put the smaller number in their head. Children should use their fingers to count how many more they have counted on to reach the larger number. Describe the situation each time using subtraction vocabulary: *Nine subtract four; nine take away four; nine minus four.*

  ▶ *Variation: start numbers can be extended to include numbers beyond ten and children can subtract using number cards 0–10.*

Feedback

Can each child remove a smaller number from a larger number and find how many are left by counting on from the smaller number?

Is anyone beginning to count on small amounts (two or three) in their head, rather than using fingers?

Who uses words such as 'minus', 'subtract', 'take away' confidently?

Counting, reading and writing numbers

Objective

Begin to write figures to 20.

Resources

▸ 0–20 number cards

What children are learning

▸ to recognize figures and name them
▸ to write figures 0–20, forming the figures in the correct way (see below)

Words you can use

digit, number, zero, one, two … twenty

Things to note

▸ Writing figures can be quite difficult for children. Common errors include reversing the figures, and writing the figures in the wrong order: 31 instead of 13.

▸ The use of felt or sandpaper figures is recommended because children develop a 'feel' for the number.

▸ Ensure that children always begin to write the figure from the correct position and move in the correct direction, as shown in the diagrams. Children often confuse the figures 3 and 5. Encourage them to trace the figures with their fingers or to write them in the air. When writing either 3 or 5 begin at the top left-hand corner and work to the right and down, returning to put the top stroke on the 5 at the end.

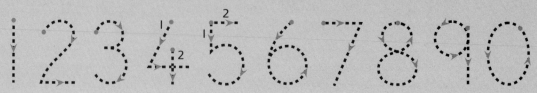

Activities

❶ **Recognize figures 0–20.**

Ask children in turn to pick a 0–20 number card and to say the number to the group. *Who has the largest number? Who has the smallest?* Ask the children to say the number names in order from zero to twenty, and for each child to hold up their card as the number name is said. *Who's got number eleven? Who's got the number that comes after eleven? What is it called? What number comes before sixteen?*

❷ Write figures 0–20.
Arrange the number cards in order and call out a number, for example *Fourteen*. Ask a child to point to the number card. Ask the children to draw this number in the air. Emphasize whether the number is made from one or two digits and whether these digits are made from straight lines, curved lines or both. Children should then copy the figure onto a piece of paper and draw that number of dots or lines next to it. Repeat as necessary, allowing children to write all the figures from 0 to 20. If children reverse their figures, help them to trace the figure correctly and guide the child's hand to draw the figure several times. It may be necessary to restrict some children to the figures 0–10 initially. Watch the way that children are forming the figures, checking the starting point and direction to ensure that children develop good habits.

Feedback

Can each child:
▸ recognize and name figures from 0 to 20?
▸ write figures to 20, forming them correctly?

Can a child show you which numbers have been written most carefully? Can they improve on any other figures?

Objective

Estimate a number beyond ten and check by counting.

Resources

▸ a selection of small items such as cubes, counters, buttons or beads
▸ a handkerchief, cloth or piece of paper

What children are learning

▸ to gain an idea of how many things there are without counting, which helps to develop a 'feel' for numbers
▸ that an estimate doesn't need to be exact but, instead, just needs to give a reasonable idea of the actual number

Words you can use

estimate, think, guess, nearly, about, close to, more than, less than, roughly

Things to note

▸ Emphasize that an estimate doesn't have to give the exact number, it is more of a 'good guess' to get a sense of how many there are. Avoid praising only estimates that are 'spot on'; instead, praise any estimate that is a 'good guess'. If children think they have to be 'spot on' they can be reluctant to estimate, preferring to count first and then pretend to have estimated the exact number.
▸ When estimating, people sometimes get clues from the arrangement of the objects, such as knowing that there are five in the arrangement shown on a dice. Looking for patterns of this type can help in making a good estimate.

Activities

❶ **Estimate more than ten objects.**

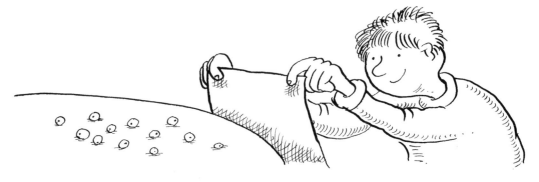

Place a handful of objects, for example twelve beads, on the table. After 3–4 seconds, cover them up with the cloth or piece of paper. *How many beads are under the cloth? Why do you think that number? Did anyone count them? Why? If there isn't time to count them what can you do?* Ask children to try to 'think' the number without counting. Collect the estimates from around the group and then uncover and count the beads. Repeat several times, giving children long enough to get a sense of the number of objects but not long enough to count them. Extend the activity to include a set of different items to estimate, for example a mixture of beads, cubes and coins. *How many things are on the table?*

❷ **Estimate using the idea of a range.**
Children can improve their estimating skills by thinking about the range within which the actual number might fall. Point to a set of books in a pile, beanbags on the floor or pencils on the table. Ask children to estimate by thinking first of a number the objects are more than, and then a number they are less than, for example 'I think there are more than eight books but less than fifteen books. My estimate is twelve.'

Feedback

Can each child give a sensible estimate of between ten and twenty objects?

Can anyone explain their estimate? For example, 'I thought there would be enough balls for the group so I think there are about eight.'

Is anyone reluctant to give an estimate without help or prompting?

Counting, reading and writing numbers

Objectives

Count in tens.
Count beyond twenty in twos.

Resources

▸ **PCM 7**, enlarged to A3 if possible
▸ interlocking cubes
▸ 10–100 number track
▸ cards marked '2', '4', '6'

What children are learning

▸ to count in tens, forwards and backwards, starting from zero or a multiple of ten
▸ to count in twos beyond twenty

Words you can use

tens, twos, count, forwards, backwards, set, twenty, thirty … one hundred

Things to note

▸ Counting forwards (and backwards) in different-sized steps helps children to gain an understanding of how numbers relate to each other. Children build up a picture of where numbers are and over time are able to visualize how many more or less a number is than another, without needing to count. Counting the 'multiples' of ten (ten, twenty, thirty …) is particularly important because, beyond twenty, all the numbers up to 100 follow the same pattern: '…ty-one', '…ty-two', '…ty-three' etc.
▸ Emphasize the connection between counting on in tens and adding ten (or counting in twos and adding two). Use a range of vocabulary to describe this: *forty plus ten; forty and ten more; forty add ten; forty and ten makes fifty altogether.*
▸ Children may fall into a pattern so that they say 'ten-ty' following 'eight-ty' and 'nine-ty'.

Activities

❶ **Count in tens.**
Show children **PCM 7**, enlarged to A3 if possible. *What are these numbers? Can anyone tell me the names of these numbers?* Revise the numbers and ask children to use the number track to count forwards and backwards in tens. Ask them to count on a certain number of tens from the start, or from any other multiple of ten: *Count on three tens from forty.* (70) *Jump from twenty to sixty. How many tens have you jumped?* (4)

❷ Count in twos.

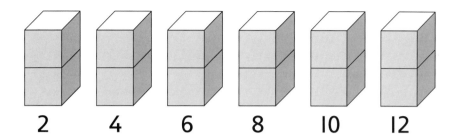

| 2 | 4 | 6 | 8 | 10 | 12 |

Ask children to join cubes together to make sticks of two. You will need lots of these. As children make the sticks, encourage them to count the number of cubes, as shown. *Can we count in twos? What do we call these numbers?* Emphasize even numbers and count in twos beyond twenty.

❸ Count in tens and twos.

Use the 10–100 number track, cards marked '2', '4' and '6' (placed face down) and the sticks of cubes to play this game. Children take turns to turn over a number card and pick up that many cubes (that is, one, two or three sticks) and add them to a central pile. When there are ten cubes (that is, five sticks) these are placed onto the 10-square. The next ten cubes are placed on the 20-square and so on. *How many twos have we here?* Count in twos, pointing to the sticks. Show the link between counting in twos up to twenty and counting in tens up to twenty. The winner can be the child who collects the cubes to reach the 50-square.

Feedback

Can each child:
▸ count in tens, forwards and backwards, starting from zero or a multiple of ten?
▸ count in twos beyond twenty?

In the number-track game, could anyone say how many twos or how many tens are on the board at any given moment?

Did anyone need help to count in twos or tens?

Adding and subtracting

Objective
Work out by counting how many more are needed to make a larger number.

Resources
▸ 0–20 number cards
▸ 0–20 number line

What children are learning
to work out by counting how many more are needed to make a larger number starting from a smaller number

Words you can use
count, more, number, one, two … twenty, set, how many?

Things to note
▸ Counting on is a strategy used for both addition and subtraction questions. For addition, counting on can be used for questions such as 4 + 3, where children count on three more places from the number 4. For subtraction this strategy can be used when finding the difference between two numbers, for example the difference between 4 and 7, where children count the number of jumps they make to reach the larger number.

▸ When counting on, children often make errors because they start counting from the number they are on, rather than from the next number, for example when counting on from three to five, children might count up 'three, four, five' and give the answer three. Encourage the children to think of the *jumps* as being the things they are counting.

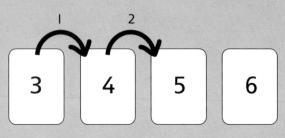

Activities

❶ Count how many more are needed to make a larger number.

▸ Put 0–5 number cards in one pile and 8–15 number cards in another pile in the middle of a table. Turn over one of the smaller cards (for example, 4). *What number is this? Can you count out that many objects for me?* Ask each child to make a set of objects (for example, four beads or four conkers) of that size. Now turn over one of the larger number cards (for example, 11). *How many more things will you need to add to your set to have eleven objects? How could we find out?* Encourage children to count on from 4 up to 11: *Think the number four in your head and count on using fingers to see how many you need to reach eleven: five, six, seven, eight, nine, ten, eleven. I am holding up seven fingers, so to get from four to eleven is seven.* Ask children to add seven objects to their set and to count them to check they have reached eleven.

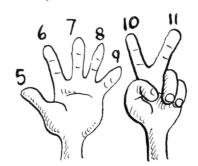

▸ Continue turning over one card from each pile and asking children to count up from the smaller number to the larger number, using their fingers to keep track.

▸ Use a 0–20 number line or track to show how this can be done by jumping on. Turn over one card from each pile; ask a child to place them by the numbers on the line and count on by jumping from the smaller number to the larger number.

Variation: use 0–20 number cards for the activity and separate them into two piles: single-digit numbers and two-digit numbers.

Feedback

Can each child work out by counting on how many more are needed to make a larger number?

Does anyone count on visually, without touching the numbers?

Did anyone need prompting about what to do?

Objectives

Use coins in role play to pay and give change.
Make simple estimates and predictions.

Resources

- ▸ 1p, 2p, 5p, 10p, 20p, 50p, £1 and £2 coins
- ▸ shop items labelled with prices of single-coin amounts
- ▸ price cards showing amounts from 1p to 5p

What children are learning

- ▸ to use coins to buy things in real situations
- ▸ to give change

Words you can use

sort, set, coins, 1p, 2p, 5p, 10p, 20p, 50p, £1, £2, pound, pence, penny, how many?, total, cost, pay, price, count, number, more, fewer, change

Things to note

- ▸ From a shop role play children can learn to appreciate many aspects related to money: the value of coins; the idea that several of one coin can be worth the same as another coin; the idea that different coins can be used to pay the same price; how to give change and so on.
- ▸ Real coins are preferred for this type of activity, although plastic coins are acceptable. If plastic coins are used, show real coins to the children to help them see how these differ from the plastic ones and to gain a feel for the weight of the coins.
- ▸ Avoid relating the size of a coin to its value by, for example, saying that 10p is bigger than a 5p so it is worth more, as this is obviously not the case for all coins.

Activities

❶ **Sorting coins.**
   Place a mixture of coins in a pile in the middle of the table. Ask children to sort them into separate piles, one pile of each type of coin.

❷ **Solve practical problems using role play.**

Set up a shop with a range of items labelled '1p', '2p', '3p', '10p', '20p', '50p', '£1' and '£2'. Choose one child to be the shopkeeper – they will need to give change where necessary (they may need support in this role). Give each child a range of coins and ask them to go shopping. Allow children time to shop and pay, asking them questions: *How much do you think it will cost? How many coins have you? Which coins are they?*

❸ **Giving change.**

Put a mixture of coins on the table, together with some price cards showing amounts from 1p to 5p. One child is designated 'banker' for the first round. Children take turns to turn over a 'price' card, for example 4p. They give the banker 10p who then gives them the correct change. Play continues around the group until all children have taken a price card. The role of banker then moves to the next child.

▶ *Variation: give each child 20p and use price cards from 1p to 19p.*

Feedback

Can each child:

▸ use coins appropriately in role play?
▸ give change for small amounts?

When giving change, note the strategies that children use and ask them to explain how they worked out the right change. For example, 'I gave 5p change because I know that five and five make ten' or 'I gave 3p change because I counted on from 7p: eight, nine, ten.'

When buying items from the shop, did anyone find it difficult to choose the right coin to pay?

The river gameboard

Supporting Number Heinemann 2000. Copying permitted for purchasing school only. This material is not copyright free.

Copy onto thin card (laminate if possible).
Cut along the dotted line and crease along fold lines.

Supporting Number Heinemann 2000. Copying permitted for purchasing school only. This material is not copyright free.

Supporting Number Heinemann 2000. Copying permitted for purchasing school only. This material is not copyright free.

Name _____ Date_____

Supporting Number Heinemann 2000. Copying permitted for purchasing school only. This material is not copyright free.

The trail gameboard

Start here

Clap

Jump

Turn around

Stand up

Touch your nose

Touch your toes

Hop

Put your tongue out

Blink

hello!

Wrinkle your nose

Cough

Touch your ear

Say 'hello'

Open your mouth

Put your finger on your lips

Nod

Supporting Number Heinemann 2000. Copying permitted for purchasing school only. This material is not copyright free.

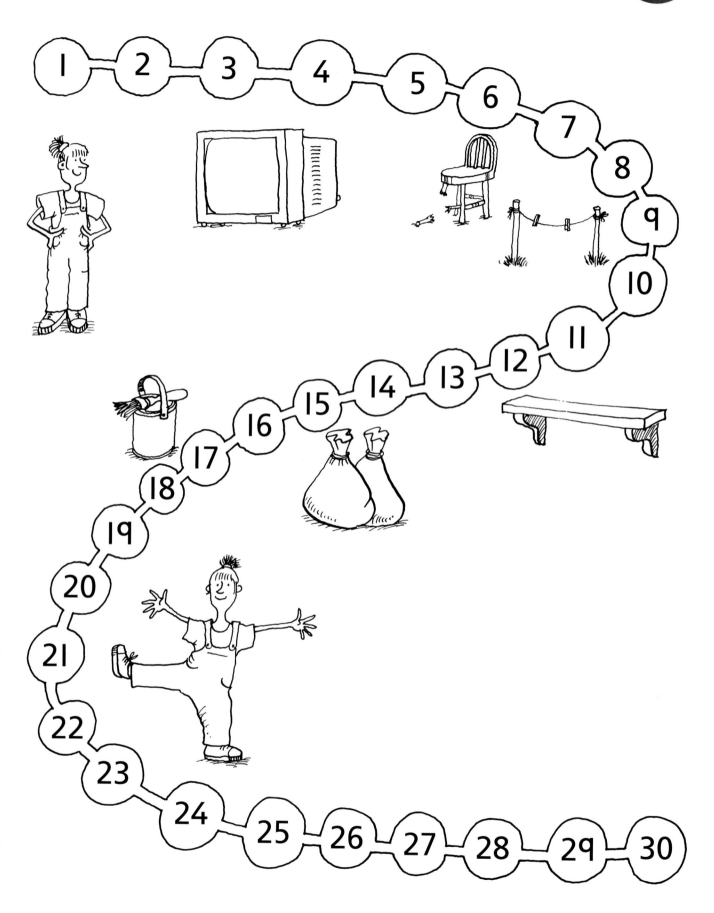

Supporting Number Heinemann 2000. Copying permitted for purchasing school only. This material is not copyright free.

Start · 10 · 20 · 30 · 40 · 50 · 60 · 70 · 80 · 90 · 100

Supporting Number Heinemann 2000. Copying permitted for purchasing school only. This material is not copyright free.

6	13	20
5	12	19
4	11	18
3	10	17
2	9	16
1	8	15
0	7	14

Supporting Number Heinemann 2000. Copying permitted for purchasing school only. This material is not copyright free.